T0340538

KOREAN BBQ & JAPANESE GRILLS

JONAS CRAMBY

PAVILION

CONTENTS

{**FOREWORD** ZEN AND THE ART OF GRILLING}

There are many similarities between Korean BBQ and Japanese grilling. It's social cooking, where bite-sized chunks of meat are grilled over small table grills and are enjoyed together with loads of simple, vegetable-based side dishes and even more ice-cold beer. But there are differences. Korean BBQ is simpler, cruder and more authentic. You would drink soju (sometimes poured straight into your beer) instead of sake, as well as a milky rice wine called makgeolli. Koreans make little salad wraps to encase their grilled meats – ssam – and the sides are neverending; the kimchi is almost more important than the type of meat you use. Japanese grilling, on the other hand, is not just about eating and drinking, it's an exercise in mindfulness too. Ingredients, crockery and tools are carefully selected, and something as simple as a piece of chicken, with some salt and fire, can – with a bit of practice, the right technique and total engagement in the present – transform into something sublime. Japanese grilling is as much about cooking the food as it is about eating it. As the American zen teacher Alan Watts said, you don't dance to 'aim at a particular spot in the room because that's where you will arrive. The whole point of the dancing is the dance'. Well, if it wasn't for the excessive consumption of alcohol and meat, it would be a damn yoga class. To really understand Japanese grilling however, we need a bit of history. And to comprehend the care and effort that is required, we need religion. But let's start with the easy part: history.

From around the Middle Ages until 1872, eating meat was prohibited in Japan. Zen Buddhism is often said to be the reason behind this ban, even though there were probably other, more practical rationale: Japan is an island with an abundance of fish along the coastline, but with a limited supply of arable land, and this land was needed to supply the inhabitants with rice. What is interesting is that Buddha wasn't a vegetarian himself; he refused to introduce bans on meat consumption, and the oldest buddhist scripture, the *Pali Canon*, retells that he ate slow-cooked pork just before he died. So, Buddha's last meal was pulled pork – just wanted to make that clear.

There were occasions when people ate game and a special force within the police, called *shinsengumi*, was said to have dispensation to eat pork, but, by and large, the Japanese diet comprised rice, vegetables and fish. When the emperor Meiji lifted the ban in 1872, in an attempt to bring Japan in line with the rest of the world, the lack of the knowledge required to prepare this new ingredient meant that it was not uncommon for people to become ill and even die from eating badly-prepared meat.

However, from the Korean neighbourhood of Tsuruhashi in Osaka, seductive smells began to spread...

During the Middle Ages, Korea had had a similar ban on meat to Japan, but when the Mongols invaded the country in the thirteenth century, this was abolished, and it wasn't long before the country developed a highly regarded pork culture. So, when meat became available in Japan, Korean immigrants began to cook their homeland's *bulgogi*, *galbi* and *samgyupsal*.

Japan's and Korea's mutual history is long, complicated and filled with racism and injustice, but – as is often the case – people still met over the dinner table. The Korean BBQ that was cooked in Tsuruhashi (see overleaf for a picture from the neighbourhood) slowly spread across Japan. Over time, it changed, becoming more Japanese, and the yakiniku was born.

Another consequence of the meat ban was that, until the twentieth century, Japan was the only country in the world that hadn't made a single native species extinct. When an animal had to be killed, the whole village mourned, and respect was so strong that they held commemorations and built shrines. Still today, Japanese slaughter houses build shrines for lost animals and most people only eat small amounts of high-quality meat.

Zen Buddhism didn't only influence what food to cook, but also how to cook it. In fact, there probably isn't a single aspect of Japanese society that hasn't been influenced by Zen philosophy, and I believe that this is what attracts so many in the West to Japanese culture. It's not the longing for meticulously sewn jeans, filter coffee that takes 30 minutes to pour, or the perfect gemstones that are sashimi, it's a longing for another kind of spirituality.

Zen Buddhism is a philosophy that is the direct opposite of Western ways of thinking. Instead of aspiring to unattainable ideals, such as eternal youth, perfection and immortality, buddhists recognise the melancholic beauty in the fact that everything ages, breaks and dies. Rather than throw away a tea cup that has broken, it is mended with golden glue that turns the cracks into beautiful detail.

Since the realization that everything is passing can be painful, it's important to always practice existing in the moment, placing no demands on either yourself or the world. This is achieved through meditation. If done correctly, almost anything can be a meditation: going for a walk or drinking a cup of tea. It is regarded as extra important to practice this sort of mindful presence when carrying out the most mundane tasks, not least when preparing food.

Dogen Zenji's *Tenzo Kyokun* – one of the most important texts of Zen Buddhism – is aimed at the head chef of a monastery. The book's simple but meticulous instructions for rinsing rice and cleaning sesame seeds are also said to be instructions for how to live your life. If you succeed in fully directing your attention and care to something as mundane as cooking, perhaps you can apply this to other aspects of life, too.

FACT FILE
HOW TO EAT THE FOOD IN THIS BOOK

The first thing you need to know about Japanese grilling is not how to cook the food, but how to eat it. If you expect that a Japanese grill night is going to be like a traditional Western dinner party, where all the food is served at the same time, everyone gets their own plate that is devoured in fifteen minutes, after which you stand around for a little boogie by the drinks table until it's time to go home – well, then you're likely to get a bit stressed out. Japanese grilling is not about filling up quickly, but about letting the meal take time. Spending time with each other. Laughing. Drinking. Nibbling. Chatting. It's literally about sharing a meal with others and I find it difficult to think of anything more pleasant in the whole world. There are however a few things to keep in mind:

STEP 1: PREPARE THE SIDES YOURSELF.
Many dishes take a long time to prepare, but are quick to eat. I would say that the food in this book works in the exact opposite way: it takes minutes to prepare, but hours to eat. Most vegetables are raw and demand a minimum amount of chopping; the sauces you basically just stir together; and the meat is cooked only once you are sat down at the table. So, when you plan a Japanese grill night, treat yourself by preparing a whole bunch of side dishes – the less you see of the set table, the better. It's good to prepare a couple of different types of meat and a load of dipping sauces and vegetables. You can combine the side dishes from the different chapters, it's not very strict. That said, you can, of course, also prepare just one or two favourites when you fancy something quick. Rice, kimchi, *samgyupsal* and some lettuce leaves make a fantastic dinner, which you will soon discover.

STEP 2: COOK THE FOOD TOGETHER.
Set a table in the garden, out on the balcony or put down a blanket in the nearest park or beach and place a table grill in the middle – since they're portable you can be pretty much where you want, even inside if you follow the instructions on page 50.

One of the best things about this food is that you can choose to make it into a complete East Asian experience, with beautiful crockery, a specially imported grill and ridiculously expensive binchotan charcoal – or you can just buy a disposable grill at the supermarket and get drunk with a few mates. It's up to you. Lay out the sides that you've prepared and have plenty of cold green tea, beer, sake or highballs at the ready. Then all you have to do is to light the grill, give a few basic instructions and get started. Reach over each other, sample the food, laugh, drink.

HOW TO EAT YAKITORI

Unlike the food in the other chapters, as a rule you don't all get involved in grilling yakitori, instead a grill chef will prepare skewer after skewer and hand them out. You don't have to do it this way of course, you can grill yakitori together on a table grill if you like.

However, a successful yakitori night is a well-planned yakitori night. You could start with *toriniku*, chicken breast, followed by *negima*, *kawa* and then *tebasaki* (see page 28). Prepare vegetable skewers in between. Then go for a mighty *tsukune* or surprise with a grilled aubergine (eggplant). You could even grill more unusual cuts of meat, such as chicken tail and heart or the kids' budgie (kidding), just for the sake of exploring. Whatever you do, the trick is to get the guests wondering about what's up next. Once you've eaten your way through the skewers, ask about the favourites and repeat these. Then do a few more repeats. If the guests are starting to crave carbs, grill a *yaki onigiri*, a grilled rice ball, or whip up a snack in the form of a *oyakodon*. Don't forget to put out a jar that you can put all the finished skewers in; it can look pretty impressive towards the end of the night.

HOW TO EAT YAKINIKU AND IZAKAYA FOOD

The most important thing to remember with yakiniku and the dishes in the izakaya chapter is that it's finger food. This means that you nibble on the food in mouthfuls using chopsticks, which sometimes can feel a bit strange for Westerners, as used to proper cutlery as we are to eating hunched over our own plates like growling, jealous dogs. But soon, you'll discover how liberating it can be to open yourself up towards your company and really SHARE a meal with people you care about. Talk about the food, complain about how spicy it is, recommend

combinations, shout loudly when you've eaten a particularly delectable piece of meat. If you serve rice with the food, it's a good idea to do so in individual bowls, and the same goes for the dipping sauces. Apart from that, it's time to let go of the fear of germs and nibble directly from all the plates of little dishes using chopsticks.

HOW TO EAT KOREAN BBQ

Korean BBQ is eaten in about the same way as yakiniku, with one big difference: you make little wraps, *ssam*, of the meat before you put it in your mouth. Exactly how this is done is shown in the illustrations on page 122.

Now, of course, there are no right or wrong ways of making a *ssam*, some just place a bit of meat in a lettuce leaf while others create vegetable tacos loaded with meat, rice, kimchi, sauce and perhaps double or triple wraps. Some even just dip the meat in a little sesame oil and then eat the lettuce like a rabbit afterwards. However, you always eat the whole wrap in one mouthful; to take a bite from it is regarded as very odd. Another thing to keep in mind is that, even if you all get involved in grilling Korean BBQ, one person usually has the main responsibility and is the person who holds the Korean meat scissors (see page 47). This person cuts up the meat into bite-sized pieces, moves already grilled meat to a cooler place and makes sure to add on more when you're running short.

A genuine Korean BBQ dinner is often introduced with *yukhoe* (see page 97) and is finished with *naengmyeon* (see page 111).

ALCOHOL-FREE GRILLING

Drinking alcohol with food is nice but, of course, not essential. For an alcohol-free grill night, I recommend cold-brewed green tea – I always have a jug at home in the fridge. It's super easy: add 1 tbsp green Japanese tea to 1 litre/1 ¾ pints/ 4 cups of water and refrigerate for 3 hours. Strain and drink. The jug can be refilled with new water twice before the leaves lose their flavour.

{**YAKITORI** GRILLED CHICKEN}

Yakitori can just as well be eaten standing under a railway arch as it can be part of a taster menu at a fancy Michelin-starred restaurant. However, wherever you eat yakitori, it's always the same dish that is served: skewered chicken, grilled over glowing embers, either dipped in BBQ sauce or rubbed with salt. It's that simple. And difficult. Yakitori isn't anything special at the same time as it's the most delicious thing in the whole world.

BUYER'S GUIDE
ALL YOU NEED FOR YAKITORI GRILLING

THE GRILL

The special grill that is used for yakitori is rectangular, to fit in many skewers side by side, and the width is designed so that only the meat lies over the embers, to avoid the wooden skewers catching fire. If you haven't got a yakitori grill, and I am going to assume you haven't (yet), you can make your own by placing two bricks on your usual outdoor grill, like in the picture below. If you grill the skewers on a table grill, soak the wooden skewers for a couple of hours before grilling.

THE CHARCOAL

The reason for almost exclusively using different kinds of binchotan charcoal for yakitori in Japan is that it's an extremely compact and hard kind of charcoal that burns for a very long time; one load often lasts for a whole evening. Since binchotan is often made from branches, it fits particularly well in a yakitori grill and burns almost without smoke and soot. It can be difficult to find binchotan charcoal outside Japan, in which case it's actually better to use charcoal briquettes rather than the standard charcoal you find at the supermarket or petrol/gas station. More charcoal info on page 86.

THE RACK

Yakitori is grilled directly over the embers, but it's also good to have a small rack of some kind to hand. Partly for grilling sides such as *yaki onigiri* on, partly for controlling the temperature on skewers that are almost done. Place them on the rack and keep a suitable distance away from the embers to finish them off. If you are grilling using a kettle grill with bricks, it might be a good idea to buy a grill net since these racks tend to have such large gaps that the food falls through. You can find grill nets at your local ironmongers.

THE SKEWERS

When it comes to skewers, *kushi* in Japanese, there are loads of different varieties that almost always come in two shapes: flat like ice-lolly sticks and round like plant-support sticks. The round ones are sharper, thinner and easier to thread the meat onto, but the flat ones are sturdier and don't roll around as much on the grill. I usually keep both varieties at home and use where they fit best. If you only find round skewers, you can use two for extra support. Remember not to buy skewers that are too long, it doesn't look great. If you can't find short skewers you can always cut them to size, or take a trip to the Asian supermarket.

TECHNIQUE
HOW TO BUTCHER A CHICKEN

In its simplest form, yakitori only contains two ingredients: chicken and salt. Therefore it's important that the quality of the chicken is as good as possible. In the last few years, many small producers have started to rear different kinds of organic chickens – talk with your butcher and buy the best chicken you can afford. When grilling yakitori for four people, it's usually enough to buy a whole chicken and complement with a few extra chicken wings, since they are always the part people want more of.

I always butcher the chicken a good time ahead, so that all you have to do is grill the skewers and drink beer once the guests have arrived. The carcass I save and cook *tare* from (see page 24), and all the offcuts I chop up and make into *tsukune* (see page 31). This way, you eat all of the poor chicken. When you've finished butchering: pull off any remaining skin on the carcass and save for *kawa* (see page 28) – the neck skin is said to be the tastiest part of the whole chicken.

I find it best to use a small, but sharp, paring knife for this job.

BREAST

Cut along the breast cartilage in the middle, along the clavicle, until the whole fillet comes off. Since chicken breast is the most boring part of the whole chicken, I actually save most of it for *tsukune* (see page 31). Peel off the skin and save for *kawa* (see page 28). You can also cut off the breast cartilage and save, it's actually really tasty to grill as it is, or finely chopped in *tsukune*, although I will understand if you don't want to.

DRUMSTICK

Make a cut in the skin on the chicken's groin. Pull the whole drumstick back until the joint comes away. Then all that is needed is to make a couple of straightforward cuts to the cartilage for the drumstick to detach fully. Be careful to avoid cutting into the bone – it will ruin the knife. Pull off the skin and save for *kawa* (see page 28).

WING

Make a cut in the skin between the wing and the body, then pull the whole wing back until the joint cracks. Make a couple of straightforward cuts to the cartilage to make it come off. Repeat for the joint between the wing and its tip. I use the middle part for *tebasaki* (see page 28) and the tip I use for *tare* (see page 24). The inner part is certainly as tasty as the one in the middle, but not as pretty, so I usually save it and grill it towards the end of the yakitori night when people as a rule are too drunk to care about such superficial things as looks.

TECHNIQUE
HOW TO
GRILL YAKITORI

Yakitori has few and simple ingredients, so it's the knack of preparing itself that makes all the difference to the end result. Depending on technique and skill, you can either end up with a grey, boring skewer without much character – or a perfectly caramelized, juicy little gold nugget.

But even if yakitori grilling is about technique and skill, I can guarantee that if you follow my tips, it will become shockingly delicious the very first time. And since it gets a bit better every time you grill, it's an incredibly satisfying way to cook.

PREPARE

Prepare the skewers before the guests arrive. Grill them in batches and serve with ice-cold drinks, such as beer or highballs. Don't rush. Yakitori is meant to be a snack to eat with drinks, so eat a lot over a long time, let it take up the whole evening. Laugh, chat, listen to music and hug each other. Always wait until it's on the grill before salting the chicken. When the chicken is almost ready, you dip it in *tare*, put it back on the grill and let the sauce caramelize for a few seconds before placing the skewers on a serving plate and drizzling over a teaspoon of *tare*.

PRIORITIZE THE SKIN

If your skewer has skin on it, it's the yakitori griller's task to prioritize this and make sure it gets perfectly cooked, super crispy and tasty. I go barking mad when people get sloppy and burn the precious skin – or, even worse, pick it off. It's NEVER okay for a person over 8 years of age to throw away crispy chicken skin, okay? So, unlike frying in a pan, you start grilling with the meat side facing down and finish with the skin side. This gives you more control over the end result. If the chicken doesn't seem grilled all the way through, grill it for a bit longer on the meat side, it doesn't matter if this gets a bit too well done as long as the skin is perfect.

DON'T RELAX

Grilling yakitori is quick and can get messed up even quicker. So always pay attention so that the skewers don't burn up, get too dry or too grey. You have to constantly roll, move or lift them when flames shoot up from the dripping fat – not least when the yakitori has skin on it.

It's a good idea to have less charcoal in one end of the grill and more in the other, so that you can move the skewers in between the heat zones as necessary.

A small grill rack that you can place the skewers on and lift away from the heat is also good. Never use a thermometer to decide whether they're done – my god, you won't have time for that – instead, poke them, touch them and trust your gut feeling. As a rule, they are always done a bit sooner than you might think – even the chicken breast should be juicy and nice.

TARE
YAKITORI SAUCE
たれ

Yakitori usually comes in two flavours: shio or tare. Shio means that the chicken is only salted, while tare simply is Japanese for dipping sauce. The tare that is used for yakitori is a sweet, salty barbecue sauce that, together with the crispy chicken and smoky grill flavour, marries into a trinity of yumminess. At Japanese yakitori restaurants, it's common that the tare is never changed, but instead refilled when needed, which means that, after time, it gets enormous depth of flavour from all the millions of chicken skewers that have been dipped into it over the years.

Serves 4

1 chicken carcass
500ml/17fl oz/generous 2 cups mirin
400ml/14fl oz/1¾ cups Japanese soy sauce
300ml/10fl oz/1¼ cups sake or white wine
1 bunch spring onions (scallions), sliced
5 garlic cloves, sliced
100g/3½oz fresh ginger, sliced

ONE   Preheat the oven to maximum temperature.

TWO   Place the chicken bones in an ovenproof dish and bake in the middle of the oven for approximately 20 minutes, until the bones have turned a beautiful dark colour.

THREE Pour the mirin, soy sauce and sake into a saucepan together with the bones. Add the spring onions, garlic and ginger. Bring to the boil over a medium heat and simmer until half of the liquid remains, about 1 hour.

FOUR Strain, pour into a clean jar with a tight-fitting lid and keep in the fridge. It will keep throughout the barbecue season, even though it probably won't last for that long.

NEGIMA

TEBASAKI

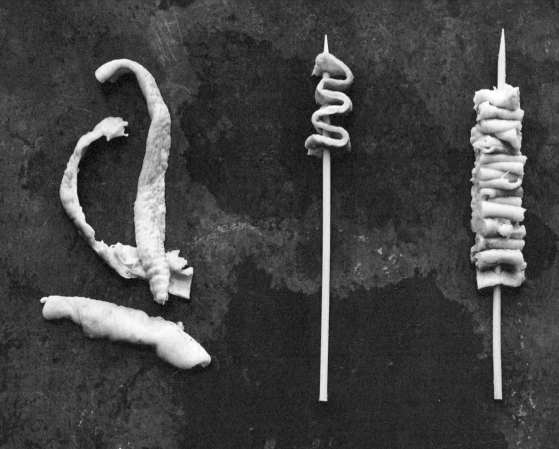

KAWA

TSUKUNE

YAKITORI
FOUR CLASSIC CHICKEN SKEWERS
焼き鳥

NEGIMA THIGHS WITH LEEK/SPRING ONION
Japanese *negi* (long onion) is difficult to find. Replace with baby leeks or spring onions.

Makes 6 skewers
2 chicken thighs, de-boned, skin removed
1–2 baby leeks/thick spring onions
  (scallions), sliced into 2-cm (¾-in) pieces
Tare, see page 24
salt

Cut the meat into 2-cm (¾-in) cubes. Thread the pieces onto skewers, layer with pieces of leek/spring onion and trim (see page 26).

TEBASAKI WINGS
Buy lots of extra wings; the two that come with the chicken won't go far.

Makes 4 skewers
8 chicken wings with skin
Tare, see page 24
shichimi togarashi (Japanese spice mix)
salt

With the underside of the middle part of the wing facing up, slice with a sharp paring knife in between the two bones that you'll feel underneath the skin. Fold out the meat so that all the skin ends up on the same side and you get two perfect bite-sized chunks on each side of the bone (see page 26). Serve with *togarashi*.

KAWA CRISPY SKIN
Pay attention when you grill *kawa*, because it's so fatty that the flames shoot up and misbehave.

Makes 4 skewers
raw chicken skin from 1 chicken
Tare, see page 24
salt

Slice the chicken skin into 1-cm (½-in) wide strips. Boil in water for 1 minute and drain on paper towels. When the skin is dry, thread it onto skewers like a concertina, then trim it into a perfect square with a sharp knife (see page 27).

TORINIKU BREAST
Always serve these to start, just to prepare the guest for what's to come.

Makes 6 skewers
1 chicken breast
1 thumb-sized chunk of wasabi,
  freshly grated (or in a tube)
salt

Cut the meat into 2-cm (¾-in) chunks and thread onto skewers. Trim so that all chunks are equally sized. Never over-grill *toriniku*, the meat should be juicy inside. Serve with a dollop of wasabi.

HOW TO GRILL YAKITORI see page 23

Negima

Kawa

Tebasaki

Toriniku

TSUKUNE
CHICKEN BALLS WITH EGG YOLK
つくね

It's a great idea to make tsukune out of all the offcuts and anything you've saved from the chicken – a super juicy, smoky chicken meatball that is dipped into egg yolk. The best tsukune is made from about equal parts lean and more fatty meat, and you have to chop everything by hand. You can use the scraps and fatty bits that you've scraped off the carcass. In Japan, it's even common to chop up the cartilage and throw that in. It gives it a special kind of chewiness that, once you've got used to it, is remarkably addictive. But you don't have to, of course.

Makes 4 skewers

about 200g/7oz chicken, equal parts lean and fatty meat
finely grated zest from ½ lemon
2 tsp sansho pepper or Sichuan pepper
Tare, see page 24
salt

To serve
4 egg yolks
4 tsp Japanese soy sauce
4 tsp sesame oil
4 tsp toasted sesame seeds

ONE Cut the chicken into chunks and then chop into a fine mince-like (ground) texture. Chop the meat all over back and forth with the knife in a checked pattern. It can take a while. Season with lemon zest, salt and sansho pepper and knead the mixture until it all holds together and becomes sticky.

TWO Press the mixture around a skewer, preferably a flat one, and shape into an American football-like shape (see page 27). Prepare for grilling by putting the loaded skewers to simmer in boiling water for 2–3 minutes.

THREE Grill according to the instructions on page 23 and serve with individual dipping bowls, each containing 1 raw egg yolk, 1 tsp soy sauce, 1 tsp sesame oil and 1 tsp toasted sesame seeds. Delicious!

KUSHIYAKI
MIXED SKEWERS
串揚げ

ASUPARAGASU GRILLED ASPARAGUS

Mayo with asparagus is a great combo – especially Kewpie which is an extra-umami-packed Japanese mayo.

Makes 4 skewers
1 tbsp white or red miso
100ml/3½fl oz/⅓ cup Kewpie mayonnaise
16 asparagus spears
1 pinch *shichimi togarashi* (Japanese spice mix)

Stir together the miso and mayo into a smooth sauce and preferably pour into a squeezy bottle. Thread 4 asparagus onto 2 skewers, as in the picture. Grill until they have coloured nicely. Squeeze over the miso mayo and top with some *shichimi togarashi*.

SHIITAKE GRILLED MUSHROOMS

Even though shiitake is the classic choice, you can grill whichever kind of mushroom you fancy.

Makes 4 skewers
8 shiitake mushrooms
1 tbsp Japanese soy sauce
1 spring onion (scallion), finely sliced
1 pinch *shichimi togarashi* (Japanese spice mix)

Remove the mushroom caps and thread 2 onto each skewer, as in the picture. Grill until the mushrooms have coloured. Brush with some soy sauce, top with a pinch of sliced spring onion and sprinkle over some *shichimi togarashi*.

UZURA NO TAMAGO GRILLED QUAILS' EGGS

These grilled quails' eggs are soft, creamy and salty – in Japan they are regarded as particularly tasty served with beer.

Makes 4 skewers
12 quails' eggs
100ml/3½fl oz/⅓ cup Japanese soy sauce
1 tbsp toasted sesame seeds

Bring some water to the boil in a saucepan, carefully add the eggs and boil for about 3 minutes. Take them out, place in ice-cold water to halt the cooking process and peel. Leave the eggs to marinate in the soy sauce for about 1 hour. Thread onto thin round skewers (3 eggs per skewer is usually a good amount) and grill until they're hot and have got some colour. Sprinkle with toasted sesame seeds and serve.

SHISHITO GRILLED CHILLIES

Shishito can be difficult to get hold of, so you can use the closely related padrón pepper.

Makes 4 skewers
12 padrón peppers
sea salt flakes

Thread 3 peppers onto each flat skewer (use 2 if you only have round ones). Grill over a high heat so that the skin darkens and blisters start to form. Sprinkle with some sea salt flakes. Serve immediately.

YAKITON
PORK SKEWERS
やきとん

At yakitori places they don't only serve chicken, sometimes you get pork too. Pork on a stick, so delicious! The simplest version of these so-called 'yakitons' is simply made up of a slice of pork belly that is treated in exactly the same way as a yakitori skewer: grill, dip in tare, grill a little bit more and put it in your mouth, accompanied by an ice-cold beer. An almost-as-simple yakiton skewer are these bacon rolls with shiso. Now, I might not be a fan of the kind of infantile bacon fetishism that has cropped up in the last few years, but this is meat candy, I admit it.

Makes 4 skewers

300g/10½oz bacon or smoked pork belly
1 bunch shiso or perilla leaves (available in Asian groceries)
Tare, see page 24 (optional)

ONE Spread out clingfilm (plastic wrap) over a work surface and place the bacon on top of it, so that each slice overlaps the next by about 1cm (½in). The better the bacon, the tastier the yakiton, but you probably get that.

TWO When all the meat has been laid out, cover the whole surface with shiso leaves and then roll it all together into a tight roll. Wrap with the clingfilm and twist the ends until you've got a neat, even cylinder. Chill in the fridge for 1 hour.

THREE Once the bacon roll has set firm, slice it into 2-cm (¾-in) thick slices. Thread 2 skewers through each slice and grill until nice and crispy. You might need to use a rack so that the rolls don't collapse. Dip in *tare* if you'd like to take the flavours to the max.

YAKI NASU
GRILLED AUBERGINE
焼きなす

Aubergine already has a smoky, sweet flavour that is enhanced both by the katsuobushi and from being grilled directly on the embers. When I grill yakitori, I almost always include an aubergine in the grill since it's a great side, but also because it creates a colder grill zone to move nearly finished skewers over to. Japanese aubergines are smaller, lighter and thinner, but you can just as well use a standard, stocky specimen.

Serves 4

1 aubergine (eggplant),
preferably Japanese
2 tbsp Japanese soy sauce
4 tsp freshly squeezed
lemon juice
2 tsp sesame oil
15g/½ oz/⅓ cup *katsuobushi*
(bonito flakes)

ONE Place the aubergine directly on the embers, there you go, just plonk it on! Turn the aubergine over from time to time so that it cooks evenly. Leave until the skin is completely black and the contents seem soft and shrunken.

TWO Take the aubergine out of the embers and cut in half lengthways. Drizzle with the soy sauce, lemon juice and sesame oil and top with *katsuobushi*.

THREE Serve immediately. Let the guests pull the aubergine flesh from the skin with their chopsticks.

YAKI ONIGIRI
GRILLED RICE BALLS
焼きおにぎり

If you've been to Japan you probably know what onigiri rice is: small stuffed rice balls that are absolutely everywhere and that are eaten a bit in the same way as we eat sandwiches or hot dogs. You eat them on the go, pack them in your kids' lunch bags when they're off on an excursion, and samurais always had some onigiri rice in their bag. Yaki onigiri means 'grilled onigiri' and is a classic side at yakitori places. It has a salty, crispy coating, a soft, smooth centre, and is a perfect carb hit when you've eaten 5,000 chicken skewers.

For 4 rice balls

200g/7oz/2 cups boiled rice,
see page 169
sesame oil, for brushing
Japanese soy sauce,
for brushing

ONE Wet your hands and shape the rice into 4 balls, or even better, into triangles, like the picture. It's the most classic shape and I managed to do it by pressing the rice in a special onigiri mould that I bought in Japan. You might be able to find the moulds in Japanese food stores.

TWO Place the onigiri on a rack and grill, making sure that all sides get coloured. Once the surface starts to crisp up, brush it with sesame oil or a little of the chicken fat that has gathered on the surface of your *tare*. Yum. Brush with a little soy sauce, a little more oil and then a little bit more soy sauce, until you have a perfectly crispy umami ball to pop in your mouth. You can also flavour the onigiri by mixing toasted sesame seeds and finely chopped nori, miso or furikake into the rice before you shape it into balls.

OYAKODON
RICE BOWL WITH CHICKEN AND EGG
親子丼

Oyakodon roughly translates as 'parent and child-bowl' and is a (somewhat bizarre) way of saying that this is a dish that contains both chicken and egg. Oyakodon is classic Japanese comfort food and at yakitori restaurants it's often served as the final dish. If you've been grilling yakitori before planning to eat oyakodon, you use charcoal-grilled chicken, of course – but you can also pan-fry the chicken if you get a craving for a quick lunch.

Serves 4

4 chicken thighs with skin on, de-boned

½ brown onion, peeled

400ml/14fl oz/1¾ cups dashi

4 tbsp mirin

4 tbsp Japanese soy sauce

4 + 4 eggs

400g/14oz/4 cups boiled rice

Soy-pickled Cucumber, see page 77

2 spring onions (scallions), finely sliced

toasted sesame seeds

salt

Dashi

6g/⅛oz kombu (about 2 x 10cm/¾ x 4in)

600ml/1 pint/2½ cups water

15g/½oz/⅓ cup *katsuobushi* (bonito flakes)

salt

ONE Dashi is a wonderfully smoky, umami-packed stock that is the base for a range of different dishes in Japanese cooking. It exists in powder form, but will, of course, be both tastier and healthier if you can face making your own. In which case: Leave the kombu to steep in a pan of cold water overnight. Place on the stove and heat until just lukewarm, it will become bitter if it starts to boil. Fish out the kombu and discard. Heat again until the bubbles start to come off the bottom of the pan, then remove from the heat and add the *katsuobushi*. Leave this to steep in the broth for 2 minutes before straining. Add salt to taste.

TWO Grill or fry the chicken thighs skin-side down, until crispy. Turn over and season with salt. Shred. Treat yourself to a piece of the crispy skin – you're human after all. Slice the onion into half moons and sauté quickly in a dry frying pan (skillet). Add the dashi, mirin and soy sauce, crack open 4 eggs and stir into the broth. Stir until the eggs have just set. Remove from the heat.

THREE Divide the rice into separate bowls, top with the dashi eggs, then arrange the chicken and soy-pickled cucumber nicely over each bowl. Top each with 1 raw egg yolk, and a sprinkling of spring onion and sesame seeds.

1.　　　　2.　　　　3.　　　　4.　　　　5.　　　　6.　　　　7.

釖

{KATANA}

8.   9.   10.   11.   12.

FACT FILE
KNIVES AND OTHER TOOLS

A good knife is not just nice to look at and fun to use, the food actually gets tastier from being cut with a sharp knife too. The Japanese art of forging has its roots in sword smithery; this is why the symbol for sword, *katana*, also can be used for knives. A Japanese handmade knife is more than just a tool, it's a piece of handicraft. Once you've used one, other knives will feel soulless in comparison. Here are the knives and tools that you need for achieving the best results when preparing the food in this book.

1. SUJIHIKI
The long, thin *sujihiki* is the Japanese version of our Western slicer and is designed to cut through de-boned raw meat with one single stroke for top-notch, beautiful slices. The single-bevelled, more traditional, *yanagiba* knife does the same job but for raw fish. You can, of course, slice beautiful slices with a long, sharp chef's knife too.

2. CHEF'S KNIFE
90 percent of all jobs in the kitchen you will do using a long chef's knife, so if you haven't got one already – invest in one now. In fact, it's the only knife that you actually need, but at the same time you only really need one pair of trousers, and who has that? An all-round knife is a shorter chef's knife; the Japanese version is called *gyuto*.

3. VEGETABLE KNIFE
A vegetable knife is perhaps not a necessity, you can easily carry out the same task with a chef's knife. But then... using a super-sharp, well-balanced vegetable knife feels a bit like having a neck-rub from someone you like. A *nakiri* is a straight-up vegetable model, perfect for quick chopping, while *bunka* (pictured) and *santoku* are for more all-round use and also a good alternative if you prefer a shorter chef's knife.

4. PARING KNIFE
I have a love affair with paring knives. Where others are attracted to big, brutal chef's knives, I get butterflies when I get to do fine jobs with a beautiful paring knife, and, in contrast to many other knives, this is a model that you sooner or later have to have – especially if you want to grill yakitori. An all-round knife is a smaller version of the chef's knife, while the Japanese paring knife is often called *petty*. Such a pretty name, *petty*.

5. UTILITY KNIFE
Occasionally you do need to open cardboard boxes or cut plastics, and if you want a super-blunt knife super-quickly, you could use your chef's knife for this. Everyone else immediately gets a simple utility knife – it could be a Mora knife, or one with a retractable blade, or, like the one in the picture, a Japanese folding knife made from carbon steel, a so-called *higonokami*.

6. OROSHIKI

Grater for finely grating things, such as daikon or wasabi. Or use a standard, extra-fine grater.

7. GRILL BRUSH

Small hand-held brush for quickly scrubbing off charred meat from the grilling rack.

8. SAIBASHI

Long chopsticks for cooking. The metal ones are used for deep-frying and grilling and come with protective wooden handles.

9. SPEED PEELER AND JULIENNE PEELER

Few things beat a good mandoline – but you can never be bothered to take it out. Better to use a simple hand-held julienne and/or speed peeler.

10. KITCHEN SCISSORS

In Korea, scissors are an indispensable tool – and I understand that. How else would you cut up *galbi* or *samgyupsal* while cooking on the grill?

11. OYSTER KNIFE

Oysters with kimchi juice is one of life's simple pleasures and to open them you need an oyster knife. Costs a few quid at the nearest fishmonger.

12. BRUSH

I usually use standard paint brushes with natural bristles for brushing grilled food.

LOOKING AFTER YOUR KNIFE

Buying an expensive knife and then throwing it into the cutlery drawer is a little bit like making a child and then keeping it in the basement. Here's how to look after your knife.

STORE IT CORRECTLY

A knife that is washed in the dishwasher and stored in the cutlery drawer will quickly become blunt. Store on a magnetic knife rack or in a knife block. Don't use for scraping vegetables from the chopping board, cutting through bones, sawing through frozen vegetables or opening packages. Always wash it by hand as soon as you've used it.

STROP IT REGULARLY

Look at a chef's knife through a microscope and you would see an edge so thin and sharp that it kind of curls up when you use the knife. In order to realign that edge regularly in between sharpenings, you usually strop it with a honing steel. This is quite tricky. An easier method is to strop it using a newspaper, see below.

SHARPEN IT

Sooner or later you will need to sharpen the knife. Machine sharpening is a common, but brutal method. Better then to learn to sharpen it yourself with a whetstone. This can be a bit tricky, so if you want to do it yourself it's a good idea to take a class. Google for classes local to you.

HOW TO STROP A KNIFE WITH A NEWSPAPER

1. Place the knife flat on a newspaper. Angle it just enough so that a couple of coins could fit underneath.

2. Move the knife away from you over the newspaper using slow, firm strokes, 30–40 times. Make sure that the whole blade gets stropped.

3. Turn over and repeat with the other side of the knife. Test the sharpness by cutting through the edge of the newspaper.

BUYER'S GUIDE
TABLE GRILLS

Contrary to what many people believe, grilling isn't a kit sport. In its most basic form, a stick and a lightning bolt is all you need to get going. So of course you don't need a table grill to make the recipes in this book. You can just as well use a kettle grill or even a frying pan (skillet).

That said, it automatically gets very cosy when everyone gathers around a small fire on the table and grills together. Small table grills are also far from the status-symbol beasts found in suburban gardens, but instead are simple, portable and in many cases so cheap that anyone could prepare a feast in parks, on balconies or even inside (see overleaf). It's also an incredibly social way of eating. Instead of having a guy in shorts begrudgingly watching over his beloved kettle grill, everyone lends a hand, you grill your own meat, reach over for sides, chat, nibble – you simply let the meal take time.

JAPANESE TABLE GRILLS

Japanska Japanese table grills, so-called *shichirins*, come in all shapes and sizes. From ashtray-sized little charcoal grills for two, to beautiful, handcrafted ceramic grills for larger groups. Whichever you prefer is a question of taste, interest and need; the important thing is that they are well insulated at the bottom so that the table doesn't catch fire. You can buy them on location in Japan (of course), online or in Asian food stores – even if the range so far is fairly limited. Try Googling 'Japanese table grill'. They're not particularly expensive either; my first Japanese table grill cost me very little.

WESTERN TABLE GRILLS

Table grilling isn't an East Asian phenomenon, there are loads of Western varieties as well. The classic disposable grill is nothing but a very simple table grill – even if it does have to be placed on top of a bunch of bricks to avoid scorching the table. Big Green Egg and other so-called kamado grills often come with a table grill option and there's an abundance of different kinds of table grills at DIY stores and ironmongers. The Lotus Grill is easy to find and, despite it being a European invention, I've seen it being used in Japan.

RACK

One problem that can arise when grilling Japanese-style is that standard grill racks have such large gaps, the little bite-sized pieces risk falling into the fire. Horrible thought. So it can be good to invest in a finer rack of Asian type. Shop around online. You can also buy grill nets from ironmongers and DIY stores for placing on top of the standard rack. In the picture, you'll also see a cast iron dome that is placed over the table grill and used for *jingisukan* especially (see page 165). You can find them in Asian food stores, often made of Teflon. They can be replaced by a wok, for example.

GRILLING TOOLS

Since everyone grills their own meat when using a table grill it can be a good idea to buy in a bunch of grill tongs. Important, however, not to buy those massive macho tools that you'll find at the DIY store. Small metal tongs for kitchen use are enough, you'll find them anywhere where they sell kitchen utensils. It's common in Japan to grill using chopsticks.

HOW TO GRILL INDOORS WITHOUT KILLING YOURSELF

Burning charcoal on the table does of course come with certain risks: burns, table linen and ties catching fire. Indeed, grilling indoors with charcoal can actually be fatal. In a poorly ventilated place, you can suffocate in the carbon monoxide fumes produced by grilling – something that unfortunately happens from time to time. So grill with responsibility and always use common sense. But I know you do.

In Asia, they're not quite as strict – there's a charcoal grill in every badly ventilated food shack, and at BBQ places the staff expertly dart in between drunken guests with glowing embers without burns, suffocations or fires happening that often. In the West, it's enough that a drunk steps on a disposable grill for the media to start reporting on the 'death grill'. So if you don't want to be a newspaper headline, and still grill safely indoors, don't use charcoal, make sure the room is well ventilated and use an electric grill or some form of gas grill. Here are three alternatives:

PORTABLE GAS GRILL
Small portable stoves with replaceable gas bottles are reasonably priced and can be found in Asian food stores. A special grill attachment can be bought as an extra. Very popular in Asia where every household has one for social cooking around the table. The disadvantage: they don't get especially hot. See picture below left.

YAKINIKU GRILL
If you want first-class grilled food all year round, there are special, highly efficient gas grills that the yakiniku places in Japan often use. They attach to gas canisters and are amazing, but so far have to be ordered from Japan. Place the grill under the kitchen fan and keep a window open. See picture below right.

YAKI AMI
If you have a gas hob at home, a simple grill alternative is to buy a *yaki ami*. Here, the gas flames heat up a net underneath a rack and you get heat radiation that is similar to a grill. Often used to grill fish, vegetables and for toasting bread in Japan, they look great. See picture right.

{YAKINIKU GRILLED MEAT}

For the Japanese, yakiniku is a very Korean way of grilling meat. For Koreans on the other hand, it's probably something very Japanese. Personally, I would say that yakiniku simply is a Japanese version of Korean BBQ that over time has developed into a style of its own. The border between yakiniku and Korean BBQ is, however, fairly flexible, so feel free to combine dishes from both chapters when planning a yakiniku night.

FACT FILE
MEAT FOR YAKINIKU

Few cuts of meat are as mythical as Japanese wagyu meat. An A5-graded beef from Matsusaka, Kobe or Omi has become the food equivalent of chrome 20-inch rims and there are insane stories about how the cows are drinking beer, getting massaged and listening to classical music in order to develop the signature marbling.

In reality, wagyu isn't THAT dramatic. The only thing wagyu actually means is 'Japanese cow' and it's a blanket term for a handful of species that have been developed in the country. In common is a genetical disposition to store more fat inside the muscle tissue. There have likely been cases of injured cows being massaged and if they've been given beer, it was probably just to increase their appetite. If you can neither afford nor source wagyu, you can grill thin slices of any kind of beef. That said, wagyu has something that no other beef has: taste. Even cheaper cuts have a buttery, nutty character that is amazing, especially on the grill.

Nowadays, many countries produce wagyu and in a range of different quality grades, and if your local butcher doesn't stock it they can probably buy it in. Almost any cut works for grilling yakiniku-style. Here are some of the most common cuts:

TOMOBARA BELLY CUTS
Tomobara is the collective term for all meat that sits around the cow's stomach, and here you will find grill favourites, such as hanger steak, flank steak, flap steak and skirt steak. The meat from this part is a bit tougher and more flavourful than from other parts – but when it comes to yakiniku that's probably all good.

KARUBI BONELESS SHORT RIBS
One of the most popular cuts of meat at a yakiniku grill and something of a personal favourite. Yes, I actually prefer slightly lower-grade short ribs to an almost white, three times more expensive A5 rib eye, as it can be just too much. These are often cut straight through and in slightly thicker pieces.

GYUTAN BEEF TONGUE
Thinly sliced beef tongue is classic grill food in Japan, and since it shares some of its qualities with wagyu, it's a cheaper alternative. Buy a fresh, not salted, piece of tongue and trim off the skin with a sharp knife. Then cut against the meat grain into approximately 5-mm (¼-in) thick slices. Rub with salt, grill, dip into *tare* and serve with freshly grated wasabi.

SAROIN BEEF STEAK
Rib eyes or beef steaks are sometimes called the cow's 'butter', and if you've seen an A5-graded piece of Matsuka wagyu you'll understand why. It's so fatty and buttery that you have to put on your reading glasses to see the meat. These parts are often eaten thickly sliced and in large portions at luxurious steak houses, while at yakiniku places you often get them as *yakishabu*, which means thinly sliced, like for *shabu shabu*.

ZABUTON CHUCK STEAK
Stew is often made from chuck but in yakınıku, the chuck steak, sometimes called the blade, is one of the most sought-after cuts because of its flavour, texture and because there isn't that much of it on a cow. Want a bargain? Find an extra-marbled piece of whole chuck steak at the meat counter as butchers often don't cut it.

Flap steak

Boneless short ribs

Beef tongue

Beef steak

Chuck steak

TECHNIQUE
HOW TO CUT
MEAT FOR YAKINIKU

To buy a large, expensive, fatty wagyu beef steak, grill it whole and serve with chips and béarnaise sauce is simply stupid – you get fat on fat on fat and it's not particularly pleasant at all.

No, wagyu is best enjoyed in moderation, with lots of lovely vegetables and so thinly sliced that the fat melts into the meat and the surface gets maximum Maillard reaction.

Large, well-marbled wagyu cuts, such as beef steak and rib eye, are often sliced thinly into neat, completely uniform slices, while leaner and more easily handled cuts, such as short ribs, flap steak and flank steak, are cut thicker, up to 1cm (½in). First-class yakiniku chefs do it all by hand and with at least as much professional skill as a sushi chef, even if for the home cook it's enough to know the three basic techniques below. Just remember to always use a super-sharp, slightly longer chef's knife, *sujishiki* or slicer, so that you can cut the meat in one single movement. Fat caps can be trimmed off before grilling since the marbling will be enough.

Arrange the sliced meat neatly on a plate and store in the fridge until it's time to grill. If you can afford and have the possibility to, it's also fantastic to be able to serve a range of different meats: start with little pieces of ox tongue and then go over to a cheaper cut, such as flank steak, then work your way up towards expensive show-off cuts like rib eye. A small piece is enough and it's not certain that the most expensive is the best. You don't need that much of each kind, just little pieces, so that you really get to experience the differences in taste and texture.

3 WAYS FOR CUTTING MEAT FOR YAKINIKU

1. To slice a thick piece of beef: cut well-chilled meat straight through in 5-mm (¼-in) thick slices. Remember to keep the knife straight and to cut in one single, long movement.

2. To slice a thinner piece of beef: cut well-chilled meat at an angle, diagonally. For neater slices, try to do it in one single, long cut.

3. For extra-thin slices: freeze the meat completely and slice using a meat slicer or, if you're ridiculously skilled, with your super-sharp knife. Or ask your butcher.

YAKINIKU
GRILLED BEEF
焼肉

Proper yakiniku is beef, usually wagyu, that is grilled in thin slices on a table grill by the guests themselves. When the meat is done it's dipped into Japanese dipping sauce, tare, and is eaten with rice and sides that sometimes still have Korean origins – and sometimes not. It's incredibly easy but, since the Japanese can't do anything half-heartedly, it's also somewhat of an art.

Serves 4

about 600g/1lb 5oz wagyu beef, or one of the alternatives from page 58

sides of your choice, pages 73–77

dipping sauces of your choice, pages 69–70

salt

ONE Prepare the sides. You can actually serve any Japanese or Korean vegetable-based side dish you like, but try to offer at least three or four options. A lot of the enjoyment in grilling yakiniku comes from letting the meal take time.

TWO Also prepare one or two different dipping sauces. Japanese dipping sauces are often very thin and simple and their job is more to enhance the flavour of the meat than to cover it with fat, spices and acidity. The most classic is *Gyu Tare* (see page 69), but it's also nice to be able to offer one, or a couple, of the other sauces in this chapter. Serve dipping sauces in individual bowls for each person.

THREE Prepare one, or more, varieties of meat by slicing it according to the instructions on page 61. Preferably present it neatly arranged on a plate. Salt the meat slightly just before you start grilling so that it doesn't get cured and so that you don't have to do it while it's cooking over the embers.

FOUR Light a table grill and place it in the middle of the beautifully set table. The more different plates and dishes, the more festive it feels. Tell your guests about the meat, the side dishes, and the dipping sauces, instruct them briefly on how to grill and eat, then let them get stuck in.

SHOGAYAKI
GINGER PORK
生姜焼き

Yakiniku isn't all about super-expensive cuts and luxury meat. Many places also complement their wagyu with so-called horumonyaki, which roughly translates as 'discarded goods' and it's a kind of literal nose-to-tail philosophy where you can order anything from cow's muzzle to bull rectum for grilling – and a lot of it is surprisingly tasty. A slightly less spectacular grill dish is shogayaki, which is a Japanese everyday favourite of thinly sliced pork in an incredibly simple ginger marinade. Eat as part of a yakiniku dinner or serve it as in many Japanese homes – with a bowl of rice and a cabbage salad.

Serves 4

500g/1lb 2oz pork collar

Ginger marinade
3½ tbsp Japanese soy sauce
3½ tbsp mirin
2 garlic cloves, grated
about 10cm/4in fresh ginger, grated

To serve
boiled rice, see page 169
1 spring onion (scallion), finely sliced
Cabbage Salad, see page 74

ONE Buy a good piece of pork collar and slice it thinly in bite-sized pieces, according to the instructions on page 61.

TWO Stir together the soy sauce, mirin, garlic and ginger into a simple marinade. Check the flavouring to make sure it really has a kick from the ginger. This is ginger pork after all. Save some marinade for serving on the side, add the meat to the remainder and leave to marinate for at least 30 minutes in the fridge, 2 hours at the most.

THREE Grill quickly and over a high heat. Shake off the marinade before placing the meat on the grill and be careful so that the soy sauce doesn't get a burnt flavour.

FOUR Eat directly from the grill or serve in a pile in a bowl of rice. In this case, pour over some of the saved marinade (that the meat hasn't been in) and top with spring onion. It's a good idea to serve it with the cabbage salad.

GYU TARE
YAKINIKU SAUCE
牛たれ

Just like the tare for yakitori and teriyaki, this super simple dipping sauce for beef is based on the ingenious sweet, salty and umami combo, mirin and soy sauce. But where the yakitori sauce is deep and broth-like, and the teriyaki sauce is sweet and sticky, this one is lighter and simpler and has a kick of acidity from the rice vinegar so the fantastic meat flavour really comes out.

Serves 4

1 garlic clove, sliced

1 thumb-sized piece of fresh ginger, sliced

200ml/7fl oz/scant 1 cup Japanese soy sauce

150ml/5fl oz/⅔ cup mirin

3½ tbsp rice vinegar

ONE Add the garlic and ginger to a saucepan together with the soy sauce and mirin. Bring to the boil, then simmer for 5 minutes before turning off the heat. Leave to stand for 20 minutes. Strain off the bits and leave to cool.

TWO Add the vinegar, pour into a nice little serving bowl and start dipping.

TARE
FOUR CLASSIC
DIPPING SAUCES
たれ

MISO MISO DIP

Punchy dip for simpler meat, something you probably won't use for the fancy cuts.

    4 garlic cloves, finely sliced
    2 tbsp red miso
    2 tbsp mirin
    1 tbsp sesame oil
    1 tbsp finely sliced spring onion (scallion)
    1 tsp toasted sesame seeds
    vegetable oil, for deep-frying

Deep-fry the garlic in oil until golden and crispy, then drain on paper towels. Mix together the miso, mirin, sesame oil, spring onion and the deep-fried garlic. Top with the sesame seeds.

PONZU CITRUS SOY DIP

You can buy ready-made ponzu, but it will, of course, taste the best if you make your own.

    2 tbsp Japanese soy sauce
    2 tbsp dashi, ready-made or see page 40
    2 tbsp freshly squeezed lemon or yuzu juice
    1 tsp mirin
    finely grated fresh daikon (optional)

Stir together the soy sauce, dashi, lemon juice and mirin in a bowl. Add a ball of finely grated daikon, if using.

SHOYU SOY DIP

The easiest way to eat your grilled meat is to treat it like sashimi: simply dip in some soy sauce with a dollop of wasabi for an extra punch. Incredibly tasty and simple, even though it might go better with simpler meat cuts.

    4 tbsp Japanese soy sauce
    1 dollop wasabi, preferably freshly grated
    some thin slices of brown onion

Pour the soy sauce into a suitable dipping bowl. Add a dollop of wasabi. Add the onion (which is mostly for garnish). Tip: if the soy sauce is too strong, you can dilute it with a bit of water or dashi. So do taste before serving.

RAN'O EGG YOLK DIP

My three favourite flavours in one: grilled meat, toasted sesame and raw egg yolk. Incredibly simple and tasty.

    4 egg yolks
    4 tsp sesame oil
    4 tsp crushed toasted sesame seeds

Place 1 egg yolk in each dipping bowl, top with 1 tsp sesame oil and sprinkle over 1 tsp sesame seeds. Done.

OKAZU
SIDES
お菜

MOYASHI NO NAMURU HOT BEANSPROUTS
Addictive beansprouts.

Serves 4
2 tbsp sesame oil
300g/10½oz fresh beansprouts
1 tbsp Japanese soy sauce
1 tsp *shichimi togarashi* (Japanese spice mix)
   or chilli flakes
1½ tsp crushed toasted sesame seeds

Heat 1 tbsp sesame oil in a wok and sauté the beansprouts quickly. They should colour and taste a little caramelized but still have a good crunch. Turn off the heat, season with the soy sauce, *togarashi* and finish with the remaining sesame oil. Sprinkle the sesame seeds on top.

EDAMAME GREEN SOY BEANS
Edamame and beer is such a classic combination that it even comes in the form of a popular Manga character – Mameshiba!

Serves 4
250g/9oz frozen edamame beans in pods
3 tbsp sesame oil
1 tsp freshly ground black pepper
½ tsp salt
½ tsp granulated sugar

Steam or boil the edamame according to the instructions on the packaging. While the beans are still hot, stir together with the sesame oil, pepper, salt and sugar. Serve immediately.

GOMADARE
GREEN SALAD WITH SESAME DRESSING
Simple green salad with the best dressing in the world!

Serves 4
1 head of lettuce
1 batch *Goma Tare*, see page 74

Tear off the salad leaves and place in iced water for 10 minutes while you stir together the dressing. Dry in a salad spinner or leave to drain thoroughly in a colander. Drizzle over the dressing to taste and serve immediately.

PA MUCHIM SPRING ONION SALAD
Simple Korean salad, perfect with grilled meat.

Serves 4
1 bunch spring onions (scallions)
2 tsp *gochugaru* or *shichimi togarashi*
   (Japanese spice mix)
2 tsp sesame oil
2 tsp Japanese soy sauce
2 tsp rice vinegar
1 tsp granulated sugar
1 tsp toasted sesame seeds

Trim, rinse and cut the spring onions into 10-cm (4-in) long pieces. Divide lengthways, fold out and discard the small section in the middle. Then slice lengthways as thinly as you can. Place in iced water for 10 minutes while you stir together the dressing ingredients. Dry in a salad spinner or leave to drain in a colander. Dress and top with the sesame seeds.

SARADA
CABBAGE SALAD
サラダ

In Japan, a large fluffy cloud of thin-thin slices of cabbage is often served as a side to shogayaki and tonkatsu (a kind of deep-fried Japanese wiener schnitzel). But it also goes well with beef. Here, it's the method, not the ingredients, that make the salad wonderfully crispy and nice. So shred thinly and don't cheat on the iced water! The carrot and the coriander might not be so authentically Japanese, but I think it's even tastier this way. The sesame dressing is one of my favourite recipes in this book and works together with any salad really, so don't miss out.

Serves 4

1 small pointed cabbage
1 carrot, finely shredded
½ bunch coriander (cilantro),
leaves only

Goma Tare – sesame dressing
2 tbsp Kewpie mayonnaise
1 tbsp sesame paste
1 tbsp red or white miso
1 tbsp water
1 tsp rice vinegar
1 tsp mirin
2 tbsp toasted sesame seeds

ONE Cut the top off the cabbage and slice it as thinly as you possibly can using a cheese slicer or, even better, a mandoline.

TWO Place the finely shredded cabbage in a bowl of iced water in order to get it super crispy, while you prepare the dressing by just stirring together all the ingredients.

THREE Spin the cabbage dry in a salad spinner (if you've got one). If not, you will have to leave it to drain thoroughly in a colander.

FOUR Mix together the cabbage, carrot and coriander and serve by placing a nice pile of ice-cold, fluffy and ridiculously crispy cabbage salad on a serving or each plate. Drizzle over some dressing just before you eat it.

KYURI
CUCUMBER SNACKS
きゅうり

CUCUMBER WITH MISO DIP

This dip favourite goes just as well with raw white cabbage, radishes or whichever crispy vegetables you can find.

   1 cucumber
   2 tbsp light miso paste
   2 tbsp light sesame paste
   1 tbsp sesame oil
   1 tbsp rice vinegar
   1 tbsp cold water
   1 tbsp crushed toasted sesame seeds

Cut the cucumber into batons. Stir together the rest of the ingredients into a sauce. Save some toasted sesame seeds for sprinkling on top. Start dipping.

CUCUMBER SMASHED

Probably more a Chinese thing. But that's okay.

   1 cucumber
   3 tbsp granulated sugar
   2 tsp salt
   1 tbsp grated garlic
   2 tbsp rice vinegar
   2 tbsp sesame oil
   2 tbsp chilli oil
   1 tsp *shichimi togarashi* (Japanese spice mix)

Place the cucumber on a chopping board and take out your fustrations on it. Cut the half-bashed cucumber into perfectly bite-sized pieces and place in a bowl. Stir together the rest of the ingredients into a dressing and pour over. Sprinkle over with *shichimi togarashi*.

CUCUMBER SOY PICKLED

Quick, classic, Japanese pickle.

   1 cucumber, finely sliced
   1 tbsp salt
   3½ tbsp rice vinegar
   1 tbsp Japanese soy sauce
   2 tsp granulated sugar
   1 tsp sesame oil
   1 tbsp toasted sesame seeds

Mix together the cucumber and salt. Leave to stand for 30 minutes before rinsing the cucumber. Stir together the vinegar, soy sauce, sugar and sesame oil for the brine and pour over. Top with the sesame seeds.

CUCUMBER WITH TABERU RAYU

This amazing Japanese chilli oil goes with almost anything, from grills to gyoza.

   1 cucumber
   5 garlic cloves, peeled
   3½ tbsp vegetable oil
   3½ tbsp sesame oil
   1 tsp *shichimi togarashi* (Japanese spice mix)
   2 tsp *gochujang* (Korean chilli paste)
   1 tbsp Japanese soy sauce
   1 tsp granulated sugar
   2 tbsp dried shrimps, chopped
   1 tbsp fresh ginger, grated

Cut the cucumber into batons. Slice the garlic and deep-fry in the vegetable oil until crispy. Drain and set aside. Add the sesame oil and the rest of the ingredients and stir. Serve over the cucumber.

GYU SANDO
BEEF SANDWICH
牛さんどいっち

At proper fancy yakiniku restaurants, it's common to finish the dinner with a simple, but luxurious, beef sandwich to either eat straight away or to take home. Since Japan is Japan they, of course, maximize the pleasure by serving it with a home-made umami ketchup. This beef sandwich is a more luxurious version of the popular katsu sandon – a sandwich with tonkatsu (pork schnitzel) and a brown sauce, similar to Worcestershire sauce, that tastes like a mix between Japanese and British umami. Incredibly delicious. You might not usually get chips with it, but I couldn't resist including an addictive, umami-packed version that I was once served at a somewhat shabby izakaya in Meguro. Still the best chips I've ever eaten.

Serves 4

500g/1lb 2oz rib eye
or beef steak
1 soft batch loaf
salt

Umami ketchup
1 brown onion, chopped
1 x 400g/14oz can tomatoes
2 tbsp tomato purée (paste)
2 tbsp Japanese soy sauce
2 tbsp Worcestershire sauce
2 tbsp fish sauce
1 tbsp cider vinegar
1 tbsp demerara sugar
cooking oil

Umami chips
40g/1½oz/⅓ cup dried anchovies
frozen chips
40g/1½oz/⅓ cup grated
Parmesan

ONE First, make the ketchup. Fry the onion in a little oil in a pan until it's soft and then add the rest of the ketchup ingredients and bring to a simmer. Blend with a hand-held blender until smooth. Simmer gently until it's reduced to ketchup consistency, it usually takes 1 hour. Season to taste with salt, leave to cool and keep in the fridge.

TWO For the umami chips, blend the anchovies into a fine umami powder. You'll find dried anchovies in Asian food stores. Make your own chips, or deep-fry frozen chips in vegetable oil at 180°C/350°F until crispy. Drain on paper towels or on a rack. Add to a bowl and mix together with the anchovy powder, Parmesan and salt, to taste.

THREE Grill room-temperature meat on a hot grill until medium-rare. Add salt and leave to rest for 10 minutes. Cut a soft batch loaf into thick slices, the fluffier the bread, the better. Toast one side of the bread slices in a frying pan (skillet). Spread umami ketchup onto the toasted sides, add the meat, place the other bread slices on top and trim off the edges. Cut the sandwiches in half and serve with the umami chips.

TECHNIQUE
HOW TO MAKE
A DONBURI

If you can't face organizing a whole night of grilling and need something quick and tasty (and Japanese) for dinner instead, you could always make a *donburi*. A Japanese *donburi*, or rice bowl, can take almost any shape and form. You can use whatever kind of meat, fish or vegetable you feel like and either add leftovers from a grilled dinner or cook it from scratch. Yes, almost any recipe in the whole book would be a good base for a *donburi*. Most *donburis*, or *don* for short, are usually made up in almost the same way: boiled rice is topped with protein, vegetables and other toppings. Dig in a couple of chopsticks, pop into your mouth and you've got everyday food for everyday luxury, folks. This is how to do it:

1. THE RICE

The rice for your *donburi* should, of course, be short-grained, preferably bought from an Asian food store. It will be tastier, of better quality and come in nicer packaging than what you'll find in the supermarket. For instructions on how to boil rice, see page 169.

2. THE PROTEIN

A *donburi* needs something meaty – though it doesn't have to come from animals. If you use pork it's called *butadon*, a *tendon* is a rice bowl topped with tempura, and in a *katsudon* the protein is *tonsaktsu* – a kind of Japanese wiener schnitzel. But you can also use teriyaki grilled salmon, like on page 161, or whichever yakitori chicken you can find – both incredibly tasty with some extra *tare*.

3. THE TOPPINGS

As with everything else, *donburis* also need something crispy and acidic. Store-bought Japanese pickles will do the trick, for example. Other good toppings are finely shredded nori, loads of sesame seeds or one of the Japanese spice mixes, *furikake* or *shichimi togarashi*. When it comes to sauce, it's a good idea to use a bit extra of whatever you used when grilling the meat. It's often enough to add a bit of soy sauce and sesame oil, or you could even go full-out with Japanese Kewpie mayonnaise or sriracha to make it extra yummy. A raw egg yolk or a poached egg is also almost a must-have. Always finish your *donburi* off with a bit of finely sliced spring onion (scallion) – it's so pretty.

Pictured is a classic gyudun *made from rice, grilled, thinly sliced beef,* gyu tare, *poached egg, toasted sesame seeds and spring onion – julienned and finely shredded. A favourite.*

備長炭

{BINCHOTAN}

FACT FILE
BINCHOTAN

When you choose charcoal for table or yakitori grilling, you want one that burns cleanly, without too much smoke or sparkling. Since you want the grill night to last a long time, you also want charcoal that does the same. And if the charcoal is both pretty and smells pleasant, it contributes to the whole experience. Here are five different kinds – from white and black Japanese *binchotan* charcoal to better briquettes.

1. BIRCHOTAN
Swedish, artisan charcoal from Kolektivet. As well as high-quality charcoal in slightly smaller pieces, especially developed for table grills, they are experimenting with developing a binchotan charcoal made from birch, wittily called 'birchotan'. For more info, see the stockist list on page 172.

2. SUMI AND OTHER QUALITY BRIQUETTES
It's actually better to table grill with briquettes than with low-quality whole charcoal. On the other hand, some briquettes contain bonding agents that can be bad for the environment and can damage your ceramic grill, so do look for briquettes with natural additives or preferably without. The Sumi charcoal pictured is relatively cheap – a Japanese high-quality briquette with a burn time of around 4 hours, which you can sometimes find at importers of Japanese food. Two similar Western products are Greek Fire, made solely from coal from leafy trees, and Kokoko, which is made from pressed coconut shells. Both can be ordered online.

3. IYO CHRYSANTHEMUM CHARCOAL
If the aesthetic experience is top priority, it's hard to beat this charcoal, named because the cut side looks like a chrysanthemum flower. The charcoal comes from Ehime in southern Japan and has been used for heating the water for traditional tea ceremonies for over 400 years. It burns cleanly and with a pleasant smell. The Amercian company Korin sells it, as do eBay and Amazon.

4. KISHUBINCHOTAN
In Japan, a so-called white binchotan from ubame oak has been produced since the Edo period. This charcoal is hardly dusty at all, has a black diamond-like cut side and is so compact that it sounds metallic. Because of its extremely long and even burn time and because it burns very cleanly and is almost completely smoke-less, it's regarded as the world's best charcoal for grilling. White bincotan always carries a stamp of origin and comes in varieties such as Tosa charcoal from the Kochi prefecture, Hyuga charcoal from Miyazaki, and – highest quality of them all – Kishu charcoal from Wakayama in south Japan – the area where the white charcoal comes from. Sadly, it's a dying craft. The masters are all very old without much new blood coming in and the ubame oak is becoming more and more rare. Within ten years, production is projected to have completely stalled.

5. ARAMURUBINCHOTAN
A cheaper, more accessible variety of binchotan is Japanese 'black charcoal', which isn't as hard as the white one and therefore a bit more dusty and doesn't burn for as long – although it still usually has a burn time of at least 5 hours. The American company Korin sells both black and white binchotan, as do eBay and Amazon.

Birchotan

Sumi

Iyo chrysanthemum

Kishu

Aramuru

TECHNIQUE
HOW TO LIGHT
BINCHOTAN CHARCOAL

The white binchotan charcoal that I write about on the previous page has its name because it is first carbonized at a low heat for a very long time and then, at the end of the process, is heated to over 1,000°C and put out with a damp blend of soil and ash, which gives it its silvery surface. Black binchotan charcoal is carbonized for a shorter time, is only heated to 600–700°C, and is then left to cool more slowly. Whether you've got hold of black or white binchotan charcoal, or one of the simpler types from the previous page, you will soon discover that you can't light this kind of quality charcoal in the same way as standard low-quality charcoal. As a rule, the longer a charcoal burns, the more difficult it is to set it alight. Proper first-class charcoal is so difficult to set alight that it would take hours to get it going with just a chimney starter and a scrunched-up newspaper. And if you've got a ceramic grill you should, of course, never use lighter fluid or other chemical fire starters, since it will destroy the grill, not to mention the environment.

There are, however, a few tricks you can try:

USE LIQUID PETROLEUM GAS

In Japan, binchotan charcoal is often set alight by placing a *hiokoshiki*, a special pan (pictured), over a gas flame. In comparison with other methods, this is quick, the charcoal will turn into perfect embers and the sticks will get such an incredible red sheen that you just want to take them out and lick them (don't do this!). You can just as well use a chimney starter and you can also do it the other way round – place the charcoal in the grill and then use a blowtorch of the more powerful kind. However, the result will not be as even and standard crème brûlée torches will not always have the power to light the super charcoal.

USE BRIQUETTES

If you don't own a blowtorch, the easier alternative is to light standard briquettes in your grill, and once they've started to glow you place your fancy charcoal straight over the briquettes. Just be prepared that it can take over an hour to get it going. You can get a quicker result if you preheat your binchotan charcoal in a chimney starter with a scrunched-up bit of newspaper underneath.

Another good tip is that if your fancy charcoal hasn't burned out when you've finished grilling, you can reuse it by smothering the embers. In Asia, there are special ceramic vessels for this purpose, but they can be difficult to get hold of, so I guess you'll have to get creative and try it out for yourself.

KOREAN

고기구이

{GOGI GUI KOREAN BBQ}

Gogi gui, aka Korean BBQ, relates to yakiniku in about the same way that swamp blues relates to rock'n'roll. Here you've got the origins. The roots. It's cruder, simpler, fiercer, and once you've got a taste for it, there's a great chance that you develop into an obsessive. And the food is incredibly easy to cook. Had there been any justice in the world, and if only they'd had slightly less complicated names, dishes such as samgyupsal and bo ssam would have been the new Friday-night tacos by now.

YUKHOE
KOREAN STEAK TARTARE
육회

This is steak tartare for people who don't like raw meat. It's nutty, garlicky, salty, sweet and with a wonderful freshness and crispness from the pear. Koreans often eat yukhoe before a grilled dinner and actually like to eat the meat on the borderline of frozen, although personally I think it's best cold, but not icy.

Serves 4

300g/10½oz beef topside

1 Korean or Chinese pear

2 garlic cloves, finely grated

2 tbsp Japanese or Korean soy sauce

2 tbsp sesame oil

1 tbsp honey

1 tbsp toasted sesame seeds, plus extra to serve

1 tbsp toasted pine nuts, plus extra to serve

1 spring onion (scallion), finely sliced, plus extra to serve

4 egg yolks

freshly ground black pepper

ONE For Korean steak tartare, you don't chop or grind the meat, but instead cut it into thin matchsticks – yes, you can actually say that you julienne the meat. To make this easier, and to make sure it's really cold, it's therefore a good idea to chuck the meat into the freezer for 2 hours before cooking.

TWO Peel, core and cut the pear into matchsticks. Place in a bowl with water and ice cubes so that it stays crispy and doesn't get brown.

THREE Cut the meat into approximately 3–4-mm (⅛-in) thick slices and then cut the slices into matchsticks of the same width. Try not to warm it up too much with your hands.

FOUR Stir the garlic, soy sauce, sesame oil and honey together into a sauce. Season to taste with pepper, and just before serving, add the sesame seeds, pine nuts and spring onion. Mix the beef together with the sauce.

FIVE Take the pear matchsticks out of the iced water and drain. Divide the pear across the plates, top with the meat and 1 egg yolk – you can also serve it as a dipping sauce on the side. Top with some extra sesame seeds, spring onion and pine nuts so that you get a bit of everything when you eat – it's heavenly.

GALBI
SHORT RIBS
갈비

Sorry rib eye, but short ribs is the best grill meat in the world. It's got a meatier flavour than hanger steak, nicer marbling than a rib eye and is at least as cheap as a skirt steak. Although it's never been a particularly traditional grill cut, it has become more common after the recent years' BBQ-boom. In Korea it is, together with *bulgogi* and *samgyupsal*, the grill meat above all, and it comes in a range of different varieties. Here are two:

WANG GALBI (TOP OF THE PICTURE)

This 'royal galbi' is the kind of short ribs that you often associate with Korean BBQ and the one I think you should go for first. A meaty chunk of ribs is trimmed and then cut into a long strip of meat that is rolled around the bone until it's time to grill. See instructions below. You can choose to serve the galbi with just a pinch of salt, *saeng galbi*, or marinate it, *yangnyeom galbi*. If so, use the marinade for *bulgogi* on page 101. Wang galbi is grilled by rolling out the meat on the grill and then cutting off the bone. Once the meat is nearly done, you cut it into bite-sized pieces so that everyone can pick at it, dip and make into little wraps.

L.A. GALBI (BOTTOM OF THE PICTURE)

L.A. galbi is a hybrid galbi that appeared among Korean immigrants in Los Angeles and that has since started to find its way back to Korea. Due to the fact that American butchers cut the meat differently to those in Korea, they had to buy their short ribs cut across the bones, so that several pieces of bone sit along the edge, in approximately 1-cm (½-in) thick slices. L.A. galbi is quick, cheap and easy to grill. Put simply, it's difficult to fail. You can find the cut at South American butchers as they butcher their meat in a similar way.

HOW TO CUT SHORT RIBS FOR GALBI

1. Cut the meat almost all the way through just above the bone. Open the meat up like a book.

2. Repeat until you've got a long strip of meat that is attached to the bone on one edge.

3. Carefully score a criss-cross pattern with the knife. Roll up the meat around the bone until it's time for grilling.

Wang galbi

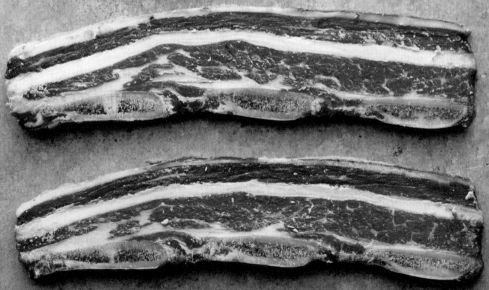

L.A. galbi

BULGOGI
MARINATED BEEF
불고기

Thinly sliced beef in a nutty, fruity marinade – this is just so good! You can make bulgogi marinade in loads of different ways, but I like to base it on pear, since it tenderizes the meat at the same time as it gives it a mild sweetness. Korean and Japanese pears are juicier and crispier than your usual pear and are therefore perfect for cooking. You'll find them in Asian food stores and quite often on the exotic fruit shelf in standard supermarkets. They are pale yellow and can be similar in shape to apples. In the worst case scenario, you could replace them with a really crispy Conference pear or similar.

Serves 4

500g–1kg/1lb 2oz–2lb 4oz beef grill meat, such as rib eye, sirloin or hanger steak

1 Korean or Japanese pear, peeled and cored

½ brown onion, peeled

4 garlic cloves, peeled

1-cm/½-in piece fresh ginger, peeled

2 tbsp Japanese soy sauce

2 tbsp toasted sesame oil

2 spring onions (scallions), coarsely chopped

To serve

Ssamjang and other toppings of your choice, see page 108

Ssam wraps of your choice, see page 107

boiled rice, see page 169

ONE Place the meat in the freezer for 1 hour and then slice it thinly and into bite-sized pieces.

TWO Blend the pear into a smooth marinade together with the onion, garlic, ginger, soy sauce and sesame oil.

THREE Put the meat and spring onions in the marinade and leave to marinate in the fridge for at least 30 minutes and up to 3 hours – too long and the meat will start to break up.

FOUR Place the meat on the table together with the toppings and grill it as you eat. If you have a tabletop griddle, it looks nice to place a pile of *bulgogi* in the middle, which you spread out as you go. If you use a rack, it's a good idea to shake off some of the marinade before placing on the grill, so that the soy sauce doesn't burn and leave a bad taste.

FIVE Eat by dipping the meat into some *ssamjang* and wrap together with other sides into a *ssam* wrap. You can eat rice added to your wrap or on the side. There are no rights or wrongs, experiment your way to the perfect mouthful.

SAMGYUPSAL
PORK BELLY
삼겹살

According to Korean grill statistics, 70 percent of Korea's population eats samgyupsal at least once a week. Once you've tried this extremely simple grill dish, it's easy to understand why. Dip a piece of crispy fried pork belly into salt and sesame oil as well as the king of condiments – ssamjang, place into a lettuce leaf or a shiso/perilla leaf – or both, add toppings of your choice and chuck into your mouth. Don't bite it off, stuff it all in! It's refined and brutal, healthy and decadent, simple and advanced, all at once.

Serves 4

500g–1kg/1lb 2oz–2lb 4oz pork belly

To serve
salt and sesame oil or *ssamjang* and other toppings of your choice, see page 108

Ssam wraps of your choice, see page 107

Kimchi of your choice, see pages 116–8

boiled rice, see page 169

ONE Slice the pork belly into approximately 1-cm (½-in) thick slices. You can choose to keep the rind or to cut it off. I like to keep it on, even though you then have to make sure it gets proper crispy when grilling.

TWO Place the meat on the table, together with the toppings and grill it all as you eat. Place a couple of slices of pork on a griddle or a rack and cook until they are almost done, then cut the meat into bite-sized pieces with kitchen scissors. Grill for a bit longer, making sure all pieces colour and get crispy.

THREE Eat by dipping the meat into either some salt and sesame oil or *ssamjang* and wrap together with other toppings of your choice into a *ssam* wrap. You can eat *kimchi* and rice added to your wrap or on the side. Don't forget to eat a piece of meat as it is with just a bit of sauce. Damn, that's tasty.

SSAM WRAPS

To stuff filling into a leaf and eat it like a taco is nothing short of ingenious. It's tasty, healthy, can be varied, and not the least, is simple – if you start eating your grilled meats like this you will soon discover that all of nature is filled with tortillas. You can wrap your grilled meat in only one of the varieties, or take two, or why not all three at the same time – there are no rights and wrongs when it comes to *ssam*. Except that you should never bite it off, but put the whole thing in your mouth, okay?

SHISO OR PERILLA LEAF

Sometimes called sesame leaf, this is not the leaf of a sesame plant, but a herb in the mint family that comes in a range of different varieties. In Japan it's called shiso, while the Latin name is perilla – which is also what it's usually called when you find it on the herb shelf in your Asian food store. It has a herby, minty tone and even if the flavour varies a little, you can use whichever kind you can find.

LETTUCE

When choosing lettuce for your *ssam* you should primarily look for different kinds of leaf lettuce, living lettuce, and green lettuce – both green and red leaves are good, but note that they shouldn't be too big and should have soft but at the same time crispy texture. Varieties such as curly lettuce or iceberg lettuce, for example, usually have too large, hard leaves to work – rocket (arugula), too small (obviously). That said you can actually make wraps out of almost anything from the vegetable counter or the garden patch. Experiment! In some parts of Korea, they wrap meat in everything from cavolo nero via pak choi (bok choy) to chicory leaves and beetroot (beet) leaves. For maximum crispiness, tear off the salad leaves and place them whole in iced water, then spin dry in a salad spinner – or let them drain thoroughly in a colander. It's a good idea to present a range of different varieties, nicely arranged on a plate. You can also place them in a press for a little while if you like them to form neat piles. That's how you usually get them at Korean BBQ places.

MU SSAM PICKLED DAIKON

For a little extra pickle kick you can make *mu ssam*, which is quick pickled Korean daikon that is coloured beautifully pink from a piece of beetroot. It's wonderful for wrapping around a piece of grilled meat. Korean daikon, *mu*, is shorter and thicker than Japanese daikon but is difficult to get hold of, so the usual daikon is okay.

Serves 4
150ml/5fl oz/⅔ cup water
3 tbsp granulated sugar
2 tbsp cider vinegar
½ raw beetroot (beet), peeled and sliced
freshly squeezed juice from ⅓ lime
½ fresh daikon, thinly sliced

Bring the water, sugar and vinegar to the boil in a pan. Add the sliced beetroot for colour and leave to cool. Once cooled down, discard the beetroot, squeeze in the lime juice and add the thinly sliced daikon. Leave in the fridge for at least 1 hour before serving.

SSAMJANG
AND OTHER
TOPPINGS
쌈장

SSAMJANG KOREAN BBQ SAUCE

Okay, I'll tell you this now: this is the best recipe in the whole book and a must if you want to make Korean BBQ. Dip the meat in this wonderful dipping sauce after grilling or add a dollop to the salad leaf when you make a parcel, whatever you want, as long as you make it. All other BBQ condiments can go and do one.

Serves 4
2 garlic cloves, finely grated
1 spring onion (scallion), finely chopped
½ white onion, finely chopped
3 tbsp chopped walnuts
2 tsp toasted sesame seeds
1 tbsp sesame oil
3 tbsp *doenjang* (Korean fermented bean paste)
1 tbsp *gochujang* (Korean chilli paste)
2 tsp honey
1 tbsp cold water

Prepare the ingredients and mix together into a wonderful sauce.

GIREUMJANG SESAME OIL AND SALT

Korean BBQ places don't always salt the meat, but instead serve it with a bowl of *gireumjang* – which is simply sesame oil with flaked salt for dipping the freshly grilled meat into.

YANGPA JANGAJJI PICKLED ONION

This pickled onion is a classic Korean condiment. Add a piece of onion to your *ssam*. Or dip the meat into the sour sauce.

Serves 4
200ml/7fl oz/scant 1 cup cold water
200ml/7fl oz/scant 1 cup Japanese soy sauce
100g/3½oz/½ cup granulated sugar
100ml/3½fl oz/generous ⅓ cup rice vinegar
2 brown onions, cut into thin wedges
freshly squeezed juice from ½ lime

Bring water, soy sauce, sugar and vinegar to the boil in a pan, until the sugar has dissolved. Leave to cool. Squeeze in lime and add the brown onion and place in the fridge. Ready to eat after 1 hour, but best after about 1 day.

GARLIC AND OTHER TOPPINGS

To serve a bowl with thickly sliced garlic can perhaps sound crude and unsophisticated, but it's amazing added to a *ssam* – well, I can't be without it at least. To mellow the flavour a little, you can grill the garlic, some even place it in a little foil bowl with a dollop of butter and put that on the grill. Other raw toppings that go well with Korean BBQ are mushrooms, sliced brown onion or chilli. Serve in a bowl and let your guests grill it when they feel like it.

Gireumjang

Ssamjang

Yangpa Jangajji

NAENGMYEON
BUCKWHEAT NOODLES
IN SLUSHIE BROTH

냉명

A Korean BBQ dinner is best finished off with a bowl of naengmyeon *– cold, chewy noodles in an iced broth. It's said that, no matter how full you are, there's always space for* naengmyeon, *since the BBQ stomach and the* naengmyeon *stomach are two different ones. That was settled a long time ago. Now I wish that I could get hold of a recipe for making* naengmyeon *from scratch, but the truth is that the kits containing noodles and a bag of ready-made broth that you can find in the fridge at your Asian food store, beat all the homemade versions that I've tried. Do, however, look for the variety called* mul-naengmyeon, *and not* bibim-naengmyeon, *since the latter comes with a chilli sauce.*

Serves 4

2 packs store-bought
naengmyeon noodles

1 Korean pear, peeled, cored
and finely shredded

1 cucumber, finely shredded

2 hard-boiled eggs, peeled
and halved

toasted sesame seeds

To serve
cider vinegar, preferably Korean

sesame oil, preferably Korean

Japanese mustard or mustard oil

ONE Put the stock packet that comes with the noodles in the freezer for a couple of hours, until the contents are cold and it contains ice crystals, a bit like a slushie.

TWO Boil the noodles according to the instructions on the packaging, then cool them in iced water. Drain.

THREE Assemble the noodles by placing some in each bowl, pour over the slushie and top with pear, cucumber and 1 hard-boiled egg half. Sprinkle over sesame seeds.

FOUR Serve with vinegar, sesame oil and Japanese mustard or mustard oil.

BAECHU KIMCHI
CLASSIC KIMCHI
배추김치

Even though there are hundreds of different kinds of kimchi, it's the fermented kimchi made from Chinese leaf cabbage that most of us are picturing in our minds when we hear the word. This kind of kimchi is not just a stinking, hot umami-bomb that makes everything it touches a little bit tastier, but it also contains bacteria cultures that are so good for you that some people think it can even cure bird flu. Furthermore, kimchi is such an important part of the Korean diet that, when they were sending off a crew of astronauts to the international space station in 2008, the government spent years and millions on research grants to develop a space-proof kimchi, that should be able to cope with both cosmic radiation and vacuum forces and that wouldn't stink out the fridge at the space station. Kimchi is simply an ingenious dish and is one of the Korean people's finest gifts to the rest of the world. So, of course, you should start making your own! But, as always when words such as fermentation and bacteria culture are involved, it's easy to think that it's complicated to make your own kimchi. The big secret is not some mysterious technique, but that it's so damn simple. Just follow a couple of basic principles and nature will do the rest – and in just a few days, a jar of completely normal cabbage is transformed into a fizzing, puffing, living creature that tastes so good that it should be bad for you, but in reality is very healthy.

Makes 2 large jars

2 Chinese leaf cabbages (about
1–1.5kg/2lb 4oz–3lb 5oz)

125g/4½oz/⅔ cup coarse sea salt

3 litres/5¼ pints cold water

1 carrot, finely shredded

4 spring onions (scallions),
finely sliced

10-cm/4-in piece fresh daikon,
finely shredded

Rice porridge

2 tbsp rice flour or wheat flour

250ml/8½fl oz/generous 1 cup
warm water

Kimchi base

10 garlic cloves, peeled

2 tbsp demerara sugar

1 brown onion, peeled

1 Korean or Japanese pear,
peeled and cored

85g/3oz/scant 1 cup *gochugaru*
(Korean red pepper flakes)

200ml/7fl oz/scant 1 cup fish
sauce, preferably Korean
anchovy sauce

1 thumb-sized piece fresh
ginger, peeled

ONE There is no perfect recipe for kimchi, it's the kind of dish that everyone has their own version of. Most of them start in the same way: by salting the Chinese leaf to give flavour and to kill bad bacteria. I think it's easiest to place the cabbage in a salt brine. Make a cut in the root of the Chinese leaf and break it into two halves. Rinse thoroughly. Remove any bad leaves and trim off a bit of the hard base, making sure that the leaves are still attached to each other. Dissolve the salt in the water in a large bucket or pan and leave the cabbage to stand for about 12 hours – I usually place a metal lid with a weight on top to press down the cabbage underneath the surface. Of course, hygiene is important when you make kimchi, so wash your hands and use thoroughly cleaned vessels.

TWO Take out the cabbage and rinse thoroughly. Taste it – if it's too salty, rinse a bit more. Drain well.

THREE To make the rice porridge, whisk the rice flour in a little of the water, add the rest, then bring to the boil, whisking until you've got a porridge. This helps the kimchi base stick to the cabbage. If you don't have rice flour, you can use wheat flour or something else that will turn into a thick roux. Cool slightly.

FOUR Blend together the kimchi base ingredients into a beautiful red paste. If you are making the quick kimchi overleaf, use it straight away; if not, stir in the rice porridge. Stir in the carrot, spring onions and daikon.

FIVE Spread the kimchi base over the cabbage. Lift the leaves, poke it into every nook and cranny, making sure that every inch is coated. Roll the cabbage into a small parcel and place in a large glass jar or plastic container with a tight-fitting lid. Make sure that the cut surface faces up and that you don't stuff it too tight – leave a little air at the top. Put the lid on.

SIX Now the kimchi is ready to ferment. It's no more complicated than leaving it at room temperature until it's fizzing when you open the lid and bubbles are rising from the bottom when you press down on the kimchi with a spoon. If you taste a little, the hot sauce should be balanced with acidity, but don't double dip. The wrong bacteria can ruin the whole batch. The fermentation phase usually takes 1–3 days, depending on how warm your home is. Then it's time to transfer your kimchi to the fridge where the fermentation will slow down. After 5 days in the fridge, the kimchi is ready. Well cooled and without any double dipping, the kimchi will keep for months.

KIMCHI
QUICK KIMCHI
김치

GOCHU SOBAGI CHILLI KIMCHI

Korean chilli can be difficult to get hold of – but any long and mild chilli will work.

Serves 4
16 long green chillies
2 tsp salt
4 tbsp Kimchi Base, see page 117
5cm/2in fresh daikon, finely shredded
1 carrot, finely shredded
1 spring onion (scallion), finely sliced
1 tbsp toasted sesame seeds

Make a cut along one side of the chillies and deseed. Sprinkle with the salt, leave to stand for 20 minutes, then rinse thoroughly and drain. Mix together the kimchi base with the daikon, carrot and spring onion. Stuff the chillies, sprinkle with sesame seeds and eat straight away or leave at room temperature overnight to start the fermentation process. Store in the fridge.

KKAKDUGI DAIKON KIMCHI

This can be eaten either shredded or diced.

Makes 1 jar
400g/14oz fresh daikon
2 tsp salt
4 tbsp Kimchi Base, see page 117

Shred the daikon or dice into 2-cm (¾-in) cubes. Sprinkle with salt, leave to stand for 20 minutes, then rinse thoroughly and drain. Mix together with the kimchi base and eat straight away or leave at room temperature overnight to start the fermentation process. Store in the fridge.

BUCHU KIMCHI GARLIC CHIVES KIMCHI

Garlic chives have a nice garlicky flavour. They can be substituted with regular chives or spring onion (scallion).

Makes 1 jar
1 bunch garlic chives
4 tbsp Kimchi Base, see page 117
1 tbsp toasted sesame seeds

Rinse the chives, pat dry and cut into 10cm (4in) pieces. Mix with the kimchi base. Top with sesame seeds and eat straight away or leave to ferment. This will happen quicker with garlic chives than with other veg, so skip the usual fermentation and put in the fridge straight away.

OISOBAGI KIMCHI CUCUMBER KIMCHI

Fresh kimchi that doesn't need to be fermented to taste fantastic.

Makes 1 large jar
2 cucumbers or 4 small ones
2 tsp salt
4 tbsp Kimchi Base, see page 117
1 carrot, finely shredded
1 spring onion (scallion), finely sliced
1 tbsp toasted sesame seeds

Cut each cucumber into quarters but keep one of the edges, so that the quarters are still attached. Sprinkle with the salt, stand for 20 minutes, then rinse thoroughly. Drain. Mix the kimchi base with the carrot and spring onion. Fill the cucumbers with the mixture, then sprinkle with the sesame seeds. Eat straight away.

Gochu sobagi

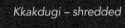

Kkakdugi – shredded

Buchu kimchi

Kkakdugi – diced

Oisobagi kimchi

BO SSAM
KOREAN
PORK WRAPS
보쌈

Every autumn (fall), an event called kimjang *takes place in Korea. It's a special period when people help each other to ferment enough kimchi to last over the winter. Afterwards, bo ssam is often served to those who have helped out – not only to help recharge their batteries with a delicious filling of pork for when they've tired themselves out, but also because there is a lot of salted Chinese leaf cabbage and fresh daikon kimchi left over to make these wonderful wraps from. Now, of course, you don't have to celebrate* kimjang *in order to eat bo ssam. You can eat it whenever and just as often as you'd like – it's perfect party food that's easy to prepare. In Korea, it's common to eat the pork boiled, but I couldn't resist giving it a crispy fried rind. Sorry, Korea.*

HOW TO MAKE A SSAM WRAP

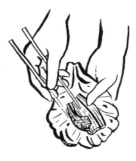

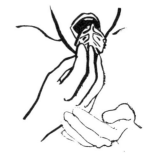

1. Place the wrap of your choice – one leaf or several – in your hand.

2. Dip the meat in *ssamjang* and place it in the wrap. Top with kimchi, rice and other fillings.

3. Fold the wrap into a small parcel and pop the whole thing in your mouth. Repeat until full.

Serves 4

1kg/2lb 4oz pork belly
2 tbsp salt
1 brown onion, sliced
6 garlic cloves, coarsely
chopped
1 thumb-sized piece fresh
ginger, sliced

Chinese leaf wraps
3 tbsp granulated sugar
3½ tbsp distilled vinegar, 12%
1 tbsp salt
1.5 litres/2½ pints/6¼ cups
cold water
500g/1lb 2oz Chinese leaves

To serve
Ssamjang, see page 108
Kkakdugi, see page 118
grilled padrón peppers
shiso or perilla leaves, or
lettuce leaves (optional)

ONE One day ahead of cooking, you will need to prepare the pork. Prick the rind all over, pat with the salt, cover and leave to stand in the fridge to soak it all up. Preheat the oven to 120°C/250°F/gas mark ½. Put the pork in an ovenproof dish together with the onion, garlic and ginger. Cover with water and place a lid on top or wrap in foil and bake in the middle of the oven for approximately 6 hours. Drain off the juices, cover and place a weight on top, and store in the fridge overnight. I usually do this by placing a smaller dish on top of the large one, then putting a heavy mortar on top.

TWO The next morning, take out your perfectly pressed meat and trim it into even more perfect rectangles. I usually make them portion-sized, approximately 10 x 3cm (4 x 1¼in). Save the offcuts for lunch, as they're incredibly tasty when fried and added to a bowl of instant ramen! Place the meat in the fridge, uncovered, so that the rind dries out before dinner – this will make it extra crispy.

THREE Prepare the Chinese leaf wraps. If you're eating *bo ssam* after you've made kimchi, make sure you save a few salted Chinese cabbage leaves. If not, it's easy to make new ones. Make a brine by mixing together the sugar, distilled vinegar, salt and water. Tear up almost a whole Chinese leaf head (it's best to avoid the inner, slightly yellow leaves) and add them to the brine. Leave them to soak for approximately 2 hours, stirring occasionally. Remove the leaves from the brine, rinse, drain and store in the fridge.

FOUR When it's time for dinner, lightly score the rind on the pork belly and grill on a low heat, skin-side facing down, until it gets really crispy. Turn over and grill the other sides of the meat. You can use a frying pan (skillet) to do this as well. Slice the meat and serve with the Chinese leaf wraps, *ssamjang*, *kkakdugi*, grilled padrón peppers and shiso/perilla leaves, if you can get hold of any. Eat by placing a shiso/perilla leaf, then meat and toppings onto a pickled Chinese leaf. You can also dash a couple of teaspoons of kimchi juice on top. It's pretty amazing.

BOKKEUMBAP
FRIED KIMCHI RICE
볶음밥

Bokkeumbap is such a cherished everyday favourite in Korea that several K-pop songs have been written about the dish. If you like kimchi, you just have to add this dish to your weekday repertoire. It's good to use kimchi that's slightly old, since it will give more flavour and umami. Bokkeumbap is a bit like a Korean hash – so don't take this recipe for gospel, instead use what you happen to have lying around in the fridge and the cupboard. If you have some grilled food left over from yesterday or an open pack of bacon, chuck that in too. Live a little!

Serves 4

250g/9oz/1¾ cups finely chopped kimchi

4 garlic cloves, finely chopped

1 brown onion, finely chopped

2 tbsp cooking oil

4 tbsp juice from kimchi

3 tbsp *gochujang*

400g/14oz/4 cups boiled rice (preferably leftovers), see page 169

2 tbsp Korean or Japanese soy sauce

2 tbsp sesame oil

4 eggs, fried

2 spring onions (scallions), finely sliced

2 tbsp toasted sesame seeds

gim or nori (toasted seaweed), shredded

ONE Fry the kimchi, garlic, onion and oil together in a frying pan (skillet) over a medium heat. Stir in the kimchi juice and *gochujang* and fry the rice in this wonderful sludge until it's warm and a little crispy – you might need to chop at it with a spatula so that the rice grains become separated. Add soy sauce to taste.

TWO Remove from the heat and stir in the sesame oil.

THREE Serve out into 4 bowls and top with 1 fried egg, some spring onions, sesame seeds and seaweed.

KIMCHI UDONG
KIMCHI NOODLES
김치우동

This dish doesn't actually have anything to do in this book. It's neither grilled nor especially authentic and I didn't even come up with the idea. Instead, it's based on one of the American magazine Bon Appetit's most cooked recipes of all time. It's far too ingenious not to include. Umami-packed Korean kimchi is fried in loads of butter and is then stirred together with udon noodles (udong in Korean) that are treated like an Italian pasta – and somehow succeeds to outshine both cuisines. A perfect weekday dish and a must if you've made your own kimchi.

Serves 4

200g/7oz/1¼ cups coarsely chopped kimchi

50g/1¾oz/3½ tbsp butter

2 tbsp *gochujang*

2–3 tbsp extra juice from kimchi

100ml/3½fl oz/generous ⅓ cup chicken or vegetable stock

500g/1lb 2oz fresh udon noodles

4 egg yolks

1 tbsp toasted sesame seeds

2 spring onions (scallions), finely sliced

salt

ONE Fry the kimchi in the butter in a frying pan (skillet) over a medium heat for a few minutes. Stir in the *gochujang*, some extra kimchi juice and the stock, and simmer together into a lovely sauce. Season to taste with salt.

TWO Boil the noodles according to the instructions on the packaging, then drain. Stir the cooked noodles into the pan with the kimchi sauce and let it all cook together quickly, as if you were making an Italian pasta dish.

THREE Serve out onto plates. Top each portion with 1 raw egg yolk, some sesame seeds and spring onions. Eat and die for a moment.

酒

{OSAKE}

FACT FILE
HOW TO TELL THE DIFFERENCE BETWEEN SHOCHU, SOJU AND SAKE

Not many other countries love Western alcoholic drinks as much as Japan. In the cities, there are nerdy natural wine places, world-class cocktail bars, enormous craft beer halls, exclusive wine bars and little secret holes in the wall where they serve Scottish whisky so rare that the competitive drinker you know would have pissed his pants if he knew. At the same time, they have a fantastic drinking culture of their own, that Westerners have been less good at embracing. But it's time to change that now. Here is a course in the basics:

SHOCHU

If Japan had a national spirit, it would actually be shochu, not sake. First of all, sake is, of course, not a spirit, and not even a wine, instead, sake is brewed in almost the same way as beer. Secondly, in Japan they sell more shochu than sake nowadays. Shochu comes in a range of different grades and can be made from everything from rice and sweet potato to barley and buckwheat – there's even shochu made from carrots! Each ingredient has its own distinctive flavour, smell and dedicated following. The alcohol content varies between 25 and 40 percent, but will usually be at the lower end of the scale.

Shochu can be enjoyed in many different ways. Those who are in the know are insistent that the high-quality stuff should be enjoyed straight up, on the rocks, with a splash of warm water, or in the form of *mizuwari*: diluted with two parts sparkling water. Personally, I'm incredibly keen on all the fun shochu cocktails and highballs that you can find at izakayas in Japan. They are refreshing, cold and rarely very sweet, and not at all as alcohol-heavy as Western cocktails. Instead, they're usually around 5 percent, about the same as beer, which means they make a perfect drink to enjoy with your meal. You can, for example, mix shochu with Hoppy, a beer-flavoured soft drink, or Calpis, which is a kind of bizarre yogurt soda. Highly recommended. Or, you make an oolong or sencha highball by mixing together shochu with iced tea of your choice and pour it over ice.

Sochu sour and Chuhai are the real classics when it comes to shochu drinks, however. This is how you make them:

SHOCHU SOUR
- 1 part shochu
- 1 part freshly squeezed lime, lemon or yuzu juice
- ½ part simple sugar syrup
- 2 parts sparkling water

Mix together the shochu, citrus juice and simple syrup in a highball glass filled with ice and top up with sparkling water.

CHUHAI

1 part shochu
1 part fruit juice of your choice
2 parts sparkling water

Mix together shochu and fruit juice in a highball glass filled with ice. Top up with sparkling water.

SOJU

Japanese shochu should not be confused with the Korean soju, which certainly is a fascinating beverage, even if it might not be regarded as something for the connoisseur. Instead, it's usually an extremely cheap, easy to get hold of distillate with an alcohol content of around 20 percent, and even though it's pretty much unknown in the West, it's the world's most sold spirit by far. In 2013, 585 million litres were sold of just one brand, and in Korea, which has the world's highest alcohol consumption per capita, the beverage makes up 97 percent of the spirit market. It's enjoyed as a shot alongside beer, in cocktails, with different kinds of flavourings, or in the form of a *somaek*, which is soju mixed with beer in the proportions 3 parts soju to 7 parts beer. And soju is even used as a cleaning product – after a long BBQ night, all you have to do is to attach a spray nozzle to the bottle and spray over the tables. Actually pretty clever.

At the same time, soju isn't downright bargain booze. Everyone drinks soju. From students to pensioners, tramps to superstars. There are even more expensive, higher quality varieties, so-called *andong soju*, which has been made from rice since the Mongols invaded the country in the 1300s and brought with them the art of distillation. Nowadays, it's more common to drink soju made from potato, sweet potato or tapioca.

SAKE

Even though sake is a rice brew and not a rice wine, as I mentioned, it's not that strange that it's usually associated more with wine than with beer or spirits. First of all, it's a beverage that's served with food with a typical alcohol content of around 10–20 percent. Just like wine, it's also a cultural beverage that has been produced for an incredibly long time, over 2,500 years. It's also a very simple product at its essence, that only contains rice, yeast and water. Depending on the soil, ingredients, water, finishing and the sake maker's other individual little choices, it develops a host of complex flavours over time. Just as with wine, it's also easy to become a sake nerd – because this is incredibly delicious stuff, at least if you avoid the cheapest varieties.

So how do you drink sake? In about the same way as you would drink a wine I'd say, together with food or for social drinking. In the West, it's common to drink sake from wine glasses, but in Japan, they usually serve it in special little sake cups. That way you finish it quicker and can pour it out for each other more frequently, which is, of course, very nice. Pouring for yourself is only if you drink on your own.

Neither do you ever 'down' sake or make 'sake bombs'; you can use soju for that. When sake first came to my home country, Sweden, people were taught that it was to be enjoyed warm, but this is quite rare and in most cases it's served nice and cold. Sake also comes in a range of different grades. *Junmai* is one of the kinds that you hear of the most, and is the mark of a high-quality sake, while *nigorizake* is a cloudy, unfiltered, cruder kind of sake that has a lot of rice flavour. A favourite.

At some izakayas, you can get it poured as in the picture, with the sake flowing over the rim and down into a little wooden box. It symbolizes abundance and hospitality and does say a thing or two about the Japanese attitude to going out: even if it's full to the brim you can always fit in a bit more.

TECHNIQUE
HOW TO SUPERCOOL YOUR BEER

For those interested in drinking, table grilling has to be the perfect way to eat, since the food doesn't just last for one or two glasses but for ten, fifteen. In Japan, it's most common to either drink sake, different kinds of highballs or a glass of foamy ice-cold industrial lager with food. Now, of course I know what the average beer lover thinks about both industrial lager and about serving beer way too cold. But there is a time and a place for everything, and to sit down after a hard week's work, with a few friends, take the first sip of ice-cold lager and slip out a long 'ahhhh', can also be a kind of umami, as they say in *Jiro Dreams of Sushi*. So even though you can drink craft beer with your food, I don't think we should be too snobby about cooling the beer properly. Not today. Please. You used to love ice-cold beer once upon a time and somewhere within you that person still exists, right?

Since Japan is Japan, a range of different varieties of ice-cold beer has appeared, from frozen beer foam that's drizzled over the beer from a soft-ice-cream machine, to beer that is served 'supercooled', below freezing point.

METHOD 1 THE BEER BUCKET
If it's summer and you're in the countryside, in a park or on the balcony, few cooling methods beat the old beer bucket. Just place a bunch of beers in a bucket or cooler bag filled with ice, a couple of litres of water and, this is important, a few tablespoons of salt. The salt will lower the temperature of the water so that the beer cools down quicker, 15 minutes is often enough.

METHOD 2 THE FREEZER
If you need an ice-cold beer right this instant and don't have any ice at home, you can always leave it in the freezer for a while. 1–2 hours will usually do it for bordering freezing beer, but it will, of course, depend on how cold your freezer is. If you want the beers to cool quicker, you could always wrap them in wet paper towels before freezing. Air doesn't actually transfer heat that well, but water does – so with the paper towel method you can have a cold beer in around 15 minutes.

METHOD 3 THE FROSTED GLASS
Sometimes it's not enough with an ice-cold beer, you want it served in a nice frosted glass as well. If you've got space in the freezer, this is easy to sort: rinse the glasses and place them in the freezer without drying them off first. Leave for about 20 minutes, then take them out, crack open a beer and pour. 'Ahhhh, umami.'

METHOD 4 THE SUPERCOOLED BEER
Supercooling is not just a term used for very cold beer, it's a scientific term too. It refers to a liquid that is below freezing but that still hasn't frozen to ice. The theory is that some vessels, like glass bottles, for example, have such a smooth surface that there isn't anywhere for the ice crystals to form. The TV programme *Mythbusters* concluded that a bottle of beer needs around 3 hours in the freezer – it varies depending on the freezer however – to get supercooled, and a fun party trick is to slam the bottle on the table and watch how it instantly freezes.

HIGHBALL
WHISKY AND SODA
ハイボール

Even though this mealtime drink sounds like a classic whisky/soda, it's got a stronger link with a Japanese tradition called mizuwari, 'mixed with water', where one part spirits is mixed with two parts water. This way of drinking comes from shochu, even though it has become popular to use other kinds of spirits as well. The first time one drinks a Japanese highball, most people probably react in the same way: 'What IS this? It tastes just like whisky diluted with sparkling water (which it rightly is).' However, after a couple of glasses, you'll soon realize how clever the mizuwari tradition actually is. Think about it. Cocktails are nice, but three are enough to get you switching off street lights with karate kicks. Beer you would be able to drink for a whole evening, but you usually fill up on beer quite quickly. Enter the humble highball, a completely unsweetened, spirit-based, thirst-quenching drink with an alcohol content similar to beer, that you can enjoy with your food. The highball is extremely easy to mix together, easy to vary and to remember, and since it's a Japanese beverage, it will, of course, get you plastered – but in a spiritual, elevated way. As the bartender Julia Momose says on the Tales of the Cocktail blog: 'The beauty of this tradition is in the simplicity. It is about being in the moment, accepting the natural way in which the ice cracks, selecting the perfect piece to be the cornerstone of the drink'.

Makes 1 highball

1 part whisky, preferably Japanese, such as Suntory or Nikka

2 parts sparkling water or soda water

ice, preferably as clear and beautiful as possible

ONE Place a large beautiful ice cube, or several small ones, in a highball glass or a beer tankard. Leave to cool the glass for a few minutes and then pour over the whisky and add another couple of ice cubes.

TWO Stir with a bar spoon to cool the whisky; according to the *mizuwari* tradition, you should stir clockwise and exactly thirteen and a half times.

THREE Top with sparkling water. Pour carefully so that you don't lose any bubbles. Stir carefully another three and a half times. Serve.

SEOUL TRAIN
AND OTHER KOREAN DRINKIN' GAMES

Korea has one of the world's most unique drinking cultures. At the same time as a night out can be as hierarchical and filled with complicated etiquette rules as the rest of society, it's often just an opportunity to let your hair down. And people do: taking an evening stroll through the university neighbourhood Hongdae in Seoul, is like witnessing with your own eyes the birth of youth culture in Haight–Ashbury 1967 or Beale Street, Memphis 1957. Thousands of beautiful, fashion-aware and extremely well behaved teenagers are shopping for Korean make-up and soft toys, dancing in groups, perfectly coordinated to the latest K-pop songs, and just sitting around at galbi places, playing drinking games, drinking soju and eating barbecue food – all this while not a single person is kicking up a fight or behaving badly. It's pretty spectacular, and just the kind of cute decadence you'll also find in the Korean neighbourhood Shin-Okubo in Tokyo or in Tsuruhashi in Osaka.

But adult Koreans like a drink too, naturally. For a quick course in Korean drinking culture, Snoop and Gangnam-style's PSY's video to the song 'Hangover' is recommended. Here, the two musicians have the table full with *anjus*, drink snacks, and spin the soju until a whirlwind appears in the bottle – which is said to mellow the flavour. PSY even cures the hangover by eating the world's best quick noodles – Shin Ramyun; plays air saxophone with a bottle of Hite beer; and makes a pretty spectacular Seoul Train – a kind of East Asian version of the submarine, where shots of soju are placed on beer glasses and then tipped over so that they fall into the beer one by one, like domino tiles (see the picture on the previous page). The same PSY has also made an instructional video to all the different ways they drink soju in Korea – from simple methods, like rolling the glass on your cheek, to more complicated methods, such as drinking three shots simultaneously – without spilling anything. He also presents a masterclass in Seoul Train, where the first shot glass is tipped by flicking a beer cap at it. Incredibly impressive. Search for 'PSY soju shot' on YouTube for further study into Korean party methods. In general, Korean drinking games are pretty silly, complicated and childish, but then so are you after a couple of shots, so it seems fitting.

NICE SWING, BOSS

Place two chopsticks on top of a glass of beer. Place a shot on top of the chopsticks and then hit these with a third chopstick with a movement similar to a golf swing, so that the shot glass plops into the beer. Say 'Nice swing, boss'. Laugh. Drink. The arrangement of a shot glass over beer on chopsticks can also be used for the closely related 'Of course, boss' – where you instead bow down so low that you hit the chopsticks with your forehead and the shot plops in.

BASKIN ROBBINS 31

The first person to play chooses if they want to count to 1, 2 or 3. When they stop, the person next to them should immediately take it up and continue to count exactly three numbers. If you count more or less than three you have to down the drink and the same goes for the person who first counts to number 31. As soon as someone has to drink, you start from the beginning again.

3-6-9

This is another counting game where each player says a number in the order that they sit. However, if the number contains the digits 3, 6 or 9, you have to be quiet and instead clap your hands – and you have to clap twice if the number is 33, 36, 39 and so on. As soon as someone goes wrong they have to drink, and then you start over from the beginning again.

007

In Korean, 007 is gong-gong-chil and this game is played as follows: the first person says 'gong' and points at another person who also says 'gong' and points at a third person who says 'chil'. This person then points at a fourth person who now has to say 'bang' – after which the two people who sit next to the person have to put up their hands. If they miss, they have to drink.

SOJU

For this game, you need a bottle of soju or another (not too strong) beverage with a screw cap. Screw off the cap and fold out one of the metal bits at the end, making sure it's still attached to the cap. Now the players take turns to try to flick the metal bit off using their index finger. The one who eventually succeeds doesn't have to drink, but everyone else has to.

TITANIC

The players pour a glass half full of beer and plop in an empty shot glass. It should float in the beer. Then they take turns to pour in soju or another (not too strong) beverage. You can add a lot or a little, that's the tactic, but the one who sinks the glass has to down it.

MANDU

This is a game for two people. Both count to three and then simultaneously stretch out both hands – at the same time as they shout out the number 0, 5, 15 or 20. Each closed hand represents a zero, while an open hand represents five, so the aim of the game is to guess what the sum of all four hands is. If both get it wrong, both drink. If both get it right, both don't have to drink. And if one person gets it wrong, they have to drink.

TAP TAP

In this game, each player takes turn to tap their glass on the table one, two or three times. If you tap once the turn goes to the person on the left, if you tap twice, the turn goes to the person on the right, and if you tap three times, the turn goes to the person two steps to the left. However, and this is when things get complicated, if the player who started taps twice and the turn goes to the right, it will continue in this direction. So if the next person taps once, the turn goes to the person sitting on the right. And vice versa. The first to make a mistake has to drink.

HORSE RACING

Here, each player has a horse with a starting number that corresponds to the order in which they sit – 1, 2, 3 and so on. The first round is played by the players tapping the table as if they were galloping horses at the same time as they, in order, shout out their starting numbers. Next, it's time to attack: the last person to shout out their starting number, directly shouts out the person they attack. For example: '5 attacks 3!', upon which this person immediately does the same, '3 attacks 1.' At the same time, everyone is galloping with their fingers on the table. And this should be QUICK, if someone shows a slight hesitation, they have to drink. As soon as someone has to drink, you start from the beginning again.

CHOPSTICKS

The person who starts asks a hypothetical, somewhat embarrassing question along the lines of: 'Who has the messiest bathroom?' or 'Who's got a crush on Byun Baek-Hyun from the K-pop group EXO?', upon which the others answer by pointing at the person of their choice with their chopsticks. The person who's got the most chopsticks pointing towards them has to drink.

{IZAKAYA BAR SNACKS}

An izakaya is more than a bar, it's a temple for the simple, unadulterated pleasure of wasting a whole evening on nibbling and drinking. And then it's not just about drinking something nice with your food. Or having some nibbles together with your beer. But the opposite. Or both. A night at the izakaya is, simply put, the perfect, non-dual meal. Or for those of you who are not so well-versed in Buddhist philosophy: this chapter is about bar food. But tasty.

YAKIYASAI
GRILLED VEGETABLES
やきやさい

NASU DENGAKU GRILLED AUBERGINE

Grilled aubergine with miso and sesame seeds.

Serves 4

2 aubergines (eggplants)

1 tbsp white or red miso

1 tbsp mirin

2cm/¾in piece fresh ginger, finely grated

Japanese soy sauce

1 tbsp toasted sesame seeds

Halve the aubergines lengthways. Score the insides. Grill, face-down, until soft. Mix the miso, mirin and ginger and brush the scored sides. Return to the grill and leave to caramelize. Add some soy sauce. Top with sesame seeds.

AVOCADO STEAK GRILLED AVOCADO

Just like how they do it at the punk rock izakaya Tatemichiya in Tokyo.

Serves 4

2 avocados, peeled and stoned

2 tbsp Japanese soy sauce

1 tsp mirin

1 tsp white or red miso

1 tsp *shichimi togarashi* (Japanese spice mix)

1 tbsp melted butter

finely shredded nori (dried seaweed)

Slice the avocado flesh into bite-sized chunks, about eight pieces per avocado. Stir the soy sauce, mirin, miso, *shichimi togarashi* and butter together into a sauce. Grill the avocado until it has coloured nicely. Top with the sauce and nori.

ENOKI BATAYAKI GRILLED MUSHROOMS

A true izakaya classic.

Serves 4

200g/7oz mixed Asian mushrooms

2 tbsp ponzu, store-bought or see page 70

2 tbsp Japanese soy sauce

2 tbsp butter

gochugaru, to taste

Clean and place the mushrooms on a sheet of foil. Add the ponzu, soy sauce and butter. Fold into a parcel. Grill for about 10 minutes, until the mushrooms have softened and turned a nice colour. Sprinkle with *gochugaru* to finish.

YAKI TOMOROKOSHI/IMO

GRILLED CORN AND/OR SWEET POTATO

Barbecue regulars with miso butter.

Serves 4

3 tbsp room temperature butter

3 tbsp white miso

1 tbsp honey

1 garlic clove, grated

4 corn on the cob and/or sweet potatoes

Japanese soy sauce

Mix the butter, miso, honey and garlic into a miso butter. Without peeling it, grill the corn, until the husks turn black. Remove and grill until the corn has cooked. Wrap the sweet potatoes in foil and grill directly on the embers for about 20 minutes, until soft. Eat with the miso butter and splash with the soy sauce for extra saltiness.

IKAYAKI
GRILLED OCTOPUS
いか焼き

Grilled octopus is a common street food at markets and festivals in Japan. This variety is both chilli hot and a proper umami bomb, as made for nibbling while you enjoy a beer. Perfect pre-snack for a Japanese grill night.

Serves 4

4 octopus tentacles

1 tbsp olive oil

2 tbsp Kewpie mayonnaise

2 tbsp sriracha

4 tbsp *katsuobushi* (bonito flakes)

2 tbsp toasted sesame seeds

salt

ONE Place the octopus tentacles in cold, salted water in a saucepan. Bring to the boil and simmer for approximately 40 minutes before turning the heat off and leaving them to cool in the water.

TWO While still lukewarm, you can pull off as much of the octopus skin as you can be bothered with; it doesn't matter if you don't get it all off.

THREE Thread the tentacles onto a round skewer each. The skewer should go in along the length of the tentacles, so each one gets straightened out when you grill it. You can prepare everything in advance up to this point.

FOUR Brush with a little oil and grill until the tentacles have got some colour and smell nice.

FIVE Pull out the skewers and cut the octopus into bite-sized pieces. Place on a serving plate and drizzle with mayo and sriracha. Top with the *katsuobushi* and sesame seeds.

OTSUMAMI
BAR SNACKS
おつまみ

In Japan, and in large parts of the rest of East Asia, it's customary to nibble on something while you drink alcohol. These kinds of drinking snacks are called otsumami – or sakana – and are more filling than our crisps and chilli nuts, but still not a proper meal since they are not served with rice. Classic otsumami dishes are edamame beans, Japanese pickles, deep-fried chicken and different kinds of dried fish, so-called himono. Eating dried fish together with beer can be a bit unusual for the Western palate, but quickly grilled and dipped in a dollop of Kewpie mayonnaise it becomes an umami bomb that's second to none.

Serves 4

100g/3½oz mixed, dried fish from the Asian food store, e.g. *atarime* (dried squid) and *eihire* (dried skate)

other snacks, such as rice crackers, wasabi peas, deep-fried nori (optional)

4 tbsp Kewpie mayonnaise

ONE Supercool your beer (see page 135), arrange the fish, other snacks (if using) and mayo on nice plates and light a table grill – the little ones that you can find relatively easy in Asian food stores are perfect for this.

TWO Tear off pieces of the dried fish and grill until they puff up and soften. Dip into the mayo. Drink a beer. Eat some other snacks. Start from the beginning again. Repeat.

YAKIZAKANA
GRILLED FISH
焼き魚

A piece of grilled fish with crispy skin, a little rice, a bowl of miso soup, grated daikon, and ponzu for dipping in, is simple East Asian soul food, the kind of food that makes you feel satisfied while still being able to move. Fresh mackerel is the favourite, of course, but you can also use salmon, cod or even varieties such as char. Do experiment, but don't forget to prioritize the skin!

Serves 4

2 descaled fish,
such as mackerel
salt

Oroshi ponzu
100ml/3½fl oz/generous ⅓ cup
ponzu, store-bought
or see page 70
1 tbsp Japanese soy sauce

Miso soup
1 litre/1¾ pints/4 cups dashi,
store-bought or see page 40
4 tbsp white or red miso
100g/3½oz silken tofu, diced
4 tbsp dried wakame (seaweed)
2 spring onions (scallions),
finely sliced

To serve
boiled rice, see page 169
125g/4½oz/scant 1 cup
grated daikon
Japanese pickles (optional)

ONE Start by preparing the fish. A smaller fish can be grilled whole, while a larger fish is filleted first. Score a couple of crosses in the skin and salt the fish. Wrap in clingfilm (plastic wrap) and leave to quick-cure in the fridge for 15 minutes.

TWO Bring the dashi for the miso soup to the boil in a pan and stir in the miso. Add the tofu, wakame and spring onions.

THREE Stir together the ponzu with the soy sauce in a bowl.

FOUR Rinse any excess salt off the fish and dry the skin thoroughly so that it gets crispy when grilling. Start grilling with the skin-side facing down and then leave to cook through with the flesh-side facing down – around 7 minutes on the skin side and 3 minutes on the other side. If you grill the fish whole, make sure you've got a cooler zone to move the fish over to, so that the fish has got enough time to cook through at the same time as the skin gets perfectly crispy.

FIVE Serve the grilled fish together with rice, the miso soup, ponzu sauce and grated daikon – which you can plop into the sauce or serve on the side, it's up to you. Some pickles are also nice, of course.

MOTOYAKI
GRILLED OYSTERS
焼カキ

Classic Japanese bar snack for both oyster lovers and those with a phobia – when you grill
the oyster it changes character and goes from something that's challenging for some to
something that's loved by most people. Well, the mayonnaise probably helps a little too.
Enjoy as part of a Japanese izakaya night or when you just want something
umami-packed and nice for your Friday beer/sake.

Serves 4

½ brown onion, finely chopped

25g/1oz shiitake or enoki
mushrooms, finely chopped

1 tbsp butter

100ml/3½fl oz/generous ⅓ cup
Kewpie mayonnaise or
other mayo

1 tsp *shichimi togarashi*
(Japanese spice mix) or standard
chilli powder

1 tbsp red miso

8 oysters in their shells

finely sliced spring onion
(scallion)

lemon wedges

salt

ONE Fry the onion and mushrooms in the butter in a frying pan
(skillet) over a medium heat until soft. Season to taste with
salt.

TWO Stir together the mayo, *shichimi togarashi* and miso. Stir in
the mushrooms and onion.

THREE Shuck the oysters and add a dollop of the mayo mixture
on top of each.

FOUR Place on the grill and grill until the filling is bubbling away
nicely. Top with a little spring onion and squeeze over
some lemon. Serve.

TERIYAKI
SALMON WITH TERIYAKI SAUCE
てりやき

Teriyaki isn't actually a dish, but a cooking technique where a sweet and salty sauce is brushed onto grilled meat, so that it gets a wonderfully tasty, caramelized glaze. Teri even means 'to shine', while yaki is Japanese for 'grilling'. The kinds of meat you use to brush with the sauce is less important, but the most common are chicken or different kinds of fish, such as salmon, mackerel or tuna. This is a quick and easy weekday dish that everyone who has ever eaten at a shabby Japanese restaurant in the West will recognize – even though the result is so much tastier if you make your own, rather than using ready-made sauce.

Serves 4

500g/1lb 2oz salmon fillet
2 tsp toasted sesame seeds
1 spring onion (scallion)

Teriyaki sauce
100ml/3½fl oz/⅓ cup Japanese soy sauce
100ml/3½fl oz/⅓ cup mirin
1 tbsp soft dark brown sugar
½ brown onion, grated
1 thumb-sized piece fresh ginger, coarsely sliced
2 garlic cloves, coarsely sliced
1 tbsp cornflour (cornstarch)

To serve
boiled rice, see page 169
sides of your choice; Japanese pickles or miso soup

ONE Bring the soy sauce, mirin and sugar for the teriyaki sauce to the boil in a saucepan. Add the onion, ginger and garlic. Reduce the heat and simmer gently for 15–20 minutes. During this time, mix the cornflour with a little water to form a paste. Strain the liquid, bring it to the boil again and add the cornflour paste while stirring, until you get a shiny sauce.

TWO Grill (or fry) the salmon fillet. Start with the skin-side facing down. Turn over and cook for less time on the meaty side. Make sure not to let the fish dry out and always aim for a crispy skin.

THREE When the salmon is nearly done, brush it generously with the teriyaki sauce. Leave to caramelize on the grill for a couple of seconds and then brush on a little bit more.

FOUR Serve the fish in portion-sized chunks topped with the sesame seeds and spring onion. Serve with rice, any sides and some extra sauce to drizzle on top.

TATAKI
QUICK GRILLED SASHIMI
たたき

Tataki is a way of cooking protein so that you simultaneously get the soft freshness of sashimi and the toasted, caramelized flavours of something grilled. The surface of a piece of meat or fish is quickly grilled while the inside is left uncooked. The method is said to have been invented in the nineteenth century by a rebellious samurai named Sakamiti Ryoma, who had seen how the strange Europeans grilled meat by the harbour in Nagasaki. Whether that's true or not, this dish is both an incredibly delicious and simple dish.

Serves 4

Tuna tataki
200g/7oz sashimi-grade tuna
1 batch Tataki Sauce, see below
1 spring onion (scallion), finely sliced
1 tsp toasted sesame seeds
salt

OR

Topside tataki
200g/7oz beef topside
1 batch Tataki Sauce, see below
4 tbsp Kewpie mayonnaise
4 shiso or perilla leaves
1 spring onion (scallion), finely sliced
1 tsp toasted sesame seeds
salt

Tataki sauce
3 tbsp ponzu, store-bought or see page 70
3 tsp sesame oil
3 tsp Japanese soy sauce

ONE Stir together the ponzu, sesame oil and soy sauce to make the tataki sauce.

TWO Trim the fish or the meat into a beautiful piece. Grill quickly over a high heat so that the surface colours properly while the inside is still completely raw. Salt carefully.

THREE For tuna tataki: Slice the fish, across the grain, into thin slices with a super-sharp knife. Arrange on a nice plate.
Top with the tataki sauce, spring onion and sesame seeds. Eat with chopsticks.

FOUR For topside tataki: Cut the meat into approximately 4 x 5cm (1½ x 2in) cubes. Mix together with the tataki sauce. Season with salt to taste. Add a dollop of Kewpie mayo onto each shiso leaf, then a pile of the diced meat. Top with the spring onion and sesame seeds. Eat like little tacos.

JINGISUKAN
GRILLED LAMB
ジンギスカン

Jingisukan is the Japanese name for Genghis Khan and the origin of the name is said to be the helmet-shaped, cast-iron dome that is used for cooking it. The meat is grilled on the dome and the meat juices drizzle down onto the vegetables that are placed in a rim around the edge. Jingisukan domes can be bought from large Japanese food stores – although a wok would do the job just as well. If so, place the veg in the middle and the meat around it.

Serves 4

½ brown onion, peeled

½ pear, preferably Japanese, peeled and cored

6 tbsp Japanese soy sauce

2 tbsp mirin

1 garlic clove and 1 thumb-sized piece fresh ginger, peeled

2 spring onions (scallions), coarsely chopped

1kg/2lb 4oz lamb chops, rib eye or shoulder

salt and ground black pepper

Tare

2 tbsp Japanese soy sauce

2 tbsp rice vinegar

1 tbsp sesame oil

1½ tsp chilli oil

To serve

brown onion, cut into wedges

beansprouts

mixed Asian mushrooms

boiled rice, see page 169

ONE Make a marinade by blending together the onion, pear, soy sauce, mirin, garlic and ginger into a smooth sauce. Add the spring onions. Slice the lamb thinly and in bite-sized pieces according to the instructions for *yakiniku* on page 61. Leave to marinate in the fridge for 1–3 hours.

TWO Stir together the ingredients for the *tare* in a bowl.

THREE Arrange the onion wedges, beansprouts and mushrooms (to serve) nicely in a bowl. If you've found a bunapi mushroom (it looks a bit like a porcini mushroom with a large stem), then slice it thinly. Score a cross in the cap of the shiitakes if you want to show off a little.

FOUR Place a grill in the centre of the table, give your guests some instructions and start grilling! The meat is placed on the dome and the onion wedges, beansprouts and mushrooms around it. Then all you have to do is eat it, as and when it's ready.

FIVE Serve with rice and the *tare* and, preferably, with large quantities of ice-cold Sapporo, since *jingisukan* originates from Hokkaido in northern Japan.

{MESHI}

TECHNIQUE
HOW TO BOIL RICE

For us Westerners, rice is often a slightly dull side, something you boil in a portion-sized bag when you can't face peeling potatoes. For a whole lot of other people out in the world, it's both by far the most important ingredient and a big food experience. In Japan, for example, a household isn't complete without a rice cooker, and a meal is not complete without a bowl of rice.

In fact, rice is so linked to eating that the actual word for rice, *meshi*, is the same as for 'meal'. People put a lot of effort into not only choosing a good rice, but also cooking it properly and eating it according to strict etiquette rules. For example, you never dip rice into soy sauce, but eat it directly from your own individual bowl. The rice bowl is lifted off the table as you eat and the chopsticks are never placed on the edge, or even worse, stuck straight down into the rice – that's associated with death, tears and teeth grinding.

Simply put, rice is serious stuff – and I understand why. The right rice, cooked in the right way, has a sublime flavour and a sticky texture that works a bit like a cushion for the taste buds to rest on while you eat other things. It's nutritious, healthy and cheap, and if you think of it as the main ingredient, instead of thinking of it as a side, you need only a minimum of additions to create a satisfying meal.

My children, for example, love rice with *gim*, dried Korean seaweed leaves brushed with sesame oil, toasted and salted. To fill a couple of *gim* leaves with some freshly cooked rice and some toasted sesame seeds is a surprisingly tasty quick dinner. Like Asian bread and butter.

A bowl of freshly cooked rice topped with some sliced Japanese, chewy pickles is also a favourite, and then there are few things that beat the combo of rice, canned tuna and Japanese Kewpie mayonnaise. Ridiculously tasty, especially in the shape of an onigiri, see page 39, with a crispy nori leaf wrapped around it. With a rice cooker, you're never far away from a satisfying weekday meal.

BOILING RICE IN A RICE COOKER

Buy a nice short-grain rice in an Asian food store – sometimes it's also called sushi rice. Rinse the rice in cold water until the water no longer gets cloudy. Leave to soak in fresh water for 30 minutes, then drain and add new water according to the instructions on your machine. Place the bowl in the rice cooker and press the button. When the light turns on, all you have to do is to lift the lid and scoff it down. It keeps warm almost forever and always gets perfectly sticky.

BOILING RICE IN A PAN

Rinse 350g/12oz/1⅔ cups short-grain rice in cold water and drain. Repeat 3–4 times until the water starts to look clear. Add fresh water and leave to soak for 30 minutes. Drain again and add 450ml/15fl oz/scant 2 cups new water before placing the pan on the stove. Cover with a lid and boil on a rolling boil for 1 minute, then reduce the heat to medium and simmer for 5 minutes, before turning the heat down to low and cooking for a further 10 minutes until all the water has been absorbed. Remove the pan from the heat and leave to stand for a further 10 minutes.

FACT FILE
HOW TO SHOP FOR ASIAN GROCERIES

At least three times in my life I've got so fed up with shopping for the same things in the same supermarket that I've just dropped the basket in panic and run away. I know it makes me sound like the crisis-suffering dad in *American Beauty*, but, hello, aren't we all him sometimes? So what should you do if you, like me, need a bit of variation from time to time?

Answer: you go to the Asian food store.

Because starting to shop there is a bit like the culinary equivalent of arranging a key party when married life is running on empty: everything is new, exciting and a bit scary again. In my favourite store, for example, they don't only sell chicken feet – they sell three different kinds of chicken feet! But it's not just more fun to shop in the Asian food store, it's cheaper and tastier and you feel a bit like Harrison Ford in *Blade Runner*. Asian food stores can be found in most larger towns and cities, and in many smaller ones all over the place, and if you don't have one where you live, you should at least not have very far to go to the closest one. Or else, there's always the internet.

What follows is a guide to the Asian groceries that I've used in this book. Those with an asterisk in front of them are things that I think you should always have in the cupboard. They're cheap, keep for a long time, and if you have them at home – and shop for fresh ingredients in a regular supermarket – you can cook about 90 percent of the dishes in this book.

ANCHOVY SAUCE
A Korean fish sauce made from, that's right, anchovies. Can be replaced with standard fish sauce of better quality – look for the ones that only list salt, water and fish on the label.

CHILLI OIL
A red, hot oil, usually sold in glass bottles. Look for ones based on sesame oil; they're a lot nicer.

CIDER VINEGAR, KOREAN
Extra tasty cider vinegar, in my opinion. Can be replaced with the standard kind.

* DASHI
Dashi is a wonderfully smoky, umami-packed stock that is the base for lots of different dishes in Japanese cooking. It can be found in powdered form, but it's a lot nicer and healthier if you can make your own, see page 40.

* DOENJANG
Thick Korean fermented bean paste – a bit like miso. Needed for making *ssamjang*, see page 108, but nice for just dipping vegetables into. Look for brown, square plastic jars.

FURIKAKE
Japanese spice mix that is similar to *shichimi togarashi* but without chilli. Usually made up of nori, sesame seeds, katsuobushi and other nice things. Nice on a bowl of freshly cooked rice.

* GOCHUGARU

Korean chilli powder that is used for kimchi but that's also used as a seasoning. Can be found both as coarse- and fine-ground varieties. Often comes in massive bags for kimchi production.

* GOCHUJANG

A thick Korean fermented chilli paste that is used for making ssamjang, see page 108, but which is also nice to eat as it is, together with grilled meat or noodles. Can be used instead of both ketchup and chilli or barbecue sauce. Look for red, square plastic jars in the store.

JAPANESE MUSTARD

Clear yellow, extra-piquant Japanese mustard. Can usually be found next to the wasabi.

KATSUOBUSHI

Thin flakes of smoked, dried tuna which dances beautifully on top of warm food, melts in the mouth and gives a fantastic umami flavour to whatever you sprinkle it over – from grilled veg and seafood to potato crisps, rice and breakfast eggs. Also called bonito flakes.

* KEWPIE MAYONNAISE

Addictive Japanese mayo in a cute bottle. Probably contains a load of glutamate, but now that's not dangerous anymore you can just keep going. Other brands of mayonnaise will yield different results, but you can substitute this with other brands if you can't find Kewpie.

* MIRIN

A sweeter version of sake that you can find as an alcohol-free version in Asian food stores. Used for loads of sauces, so good to have at home.

* MISO

Fermented Japanese soya bean paste. Wonderful in everything from the famous miso soup to caramel sauce and ice cream. Usually comes in either a red or a white variety – buy both. They keep fresh almost forever.

MUSTARD OIL

Oil made from pressed mustard seeds. Nice together with naengmyeon (see page 111).

PEAR, KOREAN OR JAPANESE

Korean and Japanese pears are juicier and crispier than standard pears. You can find them in Asian food stores and quite often on the exotic fruit shelf in supermarkets. Often called nashi pear, they are pale yellow and can be shaped a little bit like an apple.

PONZU

Dipping sauce with citrus notes which you can either make yourself, see page 70, or buy ready-made. On the whole, most Asian condiments are find to buy ready-made. But skip the sweet chilli sauce. It's the Asian equivalent of lemon pepper. Only students and body builders eat it.

* RICE VINEGAR

Vinegar based on fermented rice. The Japanese version has a mild, smooth flavour.

SANSHO PEPPER

A kind of Japanese pepper that is closely related to Sichuan pepper. Numbs the mouth in a nice way and has a citrus note.

* SESAME OIL

Often you read that 'a drop of sesame oil is enough, or else it overpowers' and that's the most stupid thing I've ever heard! You can't get too much sesame oil and a bottle is a cupboard must-have. Look for varieties that smell nutty without any bitter notes. Specialist internet stores stock fantastic Japanese artisan sesame oil, otherwise the best varieties are usually Korean.

* SESAME PASTE

Ground sesame seeds in a glass jar. Looks, and tastes, a bit like peanut butter or tahini. It's best to buy Japanese sesame paste, which is called neri goma.

* SESAME SEEDS, TOASTED

Sesame seeds can be black or white (preferably both) but always have to be toasted for maximum sesame kick. So don't mix these up with the untoasted sesame seeds that you usually find on the baking or spice shelf in standard supermarkets. Buy from the Asian store!

* SHICHIMI TOGARASHI

Japanese spice mix with lots of ingredients, from sansho and red chilli to sesame seeds and dried orange zest.

SHISO OR PERILLA LEAVES

Herb that is usually found under the name perilla in your Asian food store. See page 107.

* SHORT-GRAIN RICE

Always. Have. At home. See page 169.

* SOY SAUCE, JAPANESE OR KOREAN

Japanese soy sauce, or *shoju*, should be light, with lots of umami and not too salty. You should be able to dip a piece of raw fish into it and enjoy it – if the soy sauce is too strong, you can dilute it with a little water. There's everything from fantastic artisan Japanese soy sauce to the usual Kikkoman, but don't confuse it with dark mushroom soy sauce. Korean soy sauce is almost the same but lighter than Japanese – both can be used interchangably.

WASABI

Japanese green horseradish. Comes as fresh, in powder form and in a tube. The fresh one is, of course, far superior, but can be difficult to source.

YUZU

Japanese aromatic citrus fruit. A few specimens can find their way over when in season, otherwise it's the bottled one you'll have to go for. Can be replaced with lemon.

STOCKISTS

amazon/eBay
The two classic online marketplaces have both Japanese grills and binchotan.

chefsarmoury.com
Australian web store stocking binchotan, Japanese knives and sharpening tools, grills and accessories.

japancentre.com
Web store for essential Japanese groceries.

japaneseknifecompany.com
Web store with a very good selection of Japanese craft knives and courses in knife sharpening.

korin.com
American web store with international shipping. Stocks Japanese grills, knives, tools and binchotan, among other things.

souschef.co.uk
Online supplier of onigiri moulds, Japanese knives, Japanese and Korean ingredients.

thewasabicompany.co.uk
UK web store selling Japanese ingredients, such as ponzu, wasabi, yuzu, artisan soy sauce and nori.

INDEX

ACKNOWLEDGEMENTS

Thanks to Roland Persson for fantastic images, endless enthusiasm and for letting me light a fire in your studio.

Thanks to Maria for all the inspiration, all your hard work with the book and for eventually, somewhat reluctantly, admitting that I actually make a good kimchi.

Thanks to my children and bonus children for putting up with sampling the dishes in this book when I know that you really prefer Scan meatballs.

The publisher would like to thank Frida Green for her work on the book.

First published in the United Kingdom in 2019 by
Pavilion
An imprint of HarperCollins*Publishers*
1 London Bridge Street
London SE1 9GF

www.harpercollins.co.uk

HarperCollins*Publishers*
Macken House, 39/40 Mayor Street Upper
Dublin 1, D01 C9W8, Ireland

Copyright © Pavilion Books Company Ltd 2019
© 2017 Jonas Cramby
Original title: *Japansk grillning. Yakitori, yakiniku och koreansk BBQ*
First published by Natur & Kultur, Sweden

ISBN 978-1-911624-04-2

A CIP catalogue record for this book is available from the British Library.

10 9 8 7 6 5 4 3

Printed and bound in China by RR Donnelley APS

This book is produced from independently certified FSC™ paper to ensure responsible forest management.

For more information visit: www.harpercollins.co.uk/green